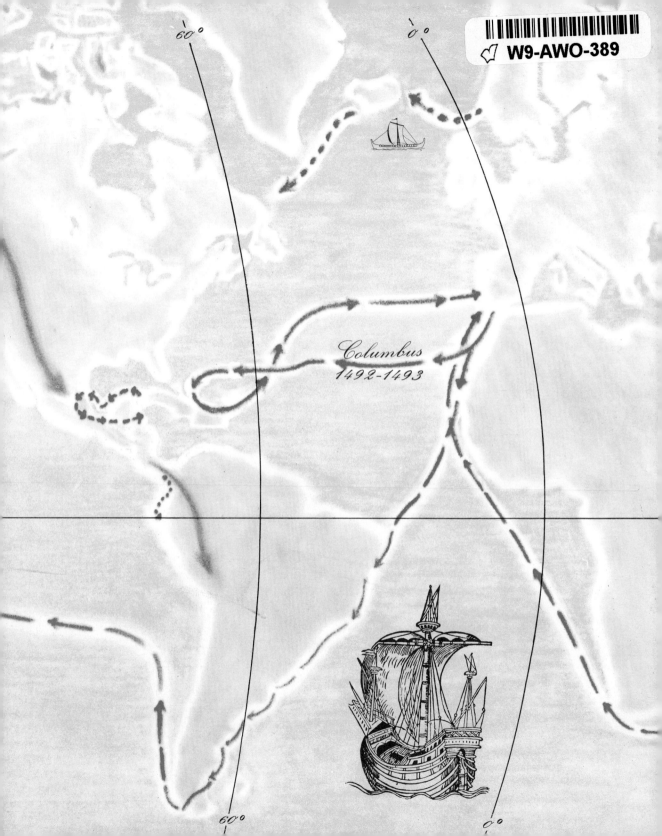

Columbus
1492-1493

PANORAMA OF WORLD ART

————

PRE-COLUMBIAN ART

and Later Indian Tribal Arts

PRE-COLUMBIAN ART

and Later Indian Tribal Arts

Texts by FERDINAND ANTON

and FREDERICK J. DOCKSTADER

HARRY N. ABRAMS, INC. Publishers NEW YORK

Front end papers:

Hannes Pixa, schematic drawing of the discovery and colonization of the Americas

Back end papers:
Abraham Ortelius, 1570 map of the world. Library, University of Leipzig

Pre-Columbian Art of Middle and South America was translated

from the German by Robert E. Wolf

Library of Congress Catalog Card Number: 68–11509

Contents

PART ONE

PRE-COLUMBIAN ART
of Middle and South America

TEXT BY FERDINAND ANTON

In 1520, when Albrecht Dürer was traveling about in the Netherlands, he saw the gifts which Moctezuma, the spiritual and religious chief of the Aztecs, had sent by Cortés to present to Emperor Charles V, and he wrote in his travel journal: "I too have seen the things brought to the Emperor from the new Land of Gold . . . and in all my life I have never seen anything which so stirred my heart as those objects. For I saw among them wonderful works of art, and I marveled at the subtle ingenuity of those men in a faraway land." This is what one of the most significant artists of the sixteenth century thought of early American art. And yet, three and one-half centuries later, the director of the Louvre refused to exhibit such objects in his museum.

The fact is that the rediscovery of early American art had to wait upon our century. It was not only the art of Africa that stimulated the imaginations of modern painters like Picasso and Paul Klee and sculptors such as Henry Moore and Jacques Lipchitz, to mention only a few, but also, and as much, Pre-Columbian art. For two thousand years we have been living with a concept of "art" that we inherited from the Greeks. Now, in the twentieth century, it has begun to lose its hold on us. Such a change in values together with the rise of a new set of values has meant that museums of art have acquired new partners—partners of equal importance—in the museums of anthropology and ethnology. Above the entrance of the Musée de l'Homme, the ethnological museum in Paris, are inscribed the words of Paul Valéry: "On him who passes by depends if I am a tomb or a treasure, if I am to remain silent or speak."

Those works of art reclaimed from the past did, indeed, begin to speak. At first, quite naturally, to artists themselves. In Dresden, Munich, and London, as in Paris, they aroused the enthusiasm of men who, in their own ways, were preparing a revolution in Western art. Many a textile pattern from ancient Peru made its way into the watercolors of Paul Klee. In many statues from the time before America was discovered can be found forms similar to those in Pablo Picasso's paintings and ceramics. The great English sculptor Henry Moore has told how he could never find the courage to create a "negative space," a hollow void within a closed form, until he had studied the Mexican sculpture in the British Museum.

Because Europe was beginning to recognize the artistic value of those objects that had survived from the time before history, the relatively young countries of Latin America, which had only recently become independent of the Spanish or Portuguese crown, were encouraged in their efforts to explore their own pasts. In Mexico alone, more than twelve thousand medium- and large-sized ancient settlements have been studied; in Peru and Bolivia something like half that number.

At the time Columbus discovered the Western Hemisphere and called its people Indians under the impression that he had reached India, there must have been between forty and forty-five million inhabitants. A French ethnologist has singled out no fewer than 123 linguistic families whose interrelationships are by no means simple. Like the languages of the New World, so too its art reveals an extraordinary diversity of aspects, forms, and techniques. In the age that concerns us here, intellectual and cultural development was centered in Mexico, Guatemala, and some parts of the neighboring regions, along with the Central Andes of Peru and Bolivia. The full development of the lands in between, those called the Lands of Gold, was cut short by the Spanish Conquest. But their artistic legacy is worthy of standing alongside the achievements of the major higher civilizations, as are also those of the so-called primitives of our own time which are surveyed at the end of this book by a great authority in this field, Dr. Frederick J. Dockstader, whose contribution unfortunately, because of limitations of space, cannot be as large as its merits.

Reality for ancient Mexico, as Paul Westheim put it, lay in the myths it lived by. This is just as true of the other Indian cultures. Most religious systems are concerned with the morally good, with the conflict between good and evil. Not so those of the early peoples of America. Their gods were conceived as embodiments of cosmic forces. For that reason, there was no separation between good and evil, because the god who made the long-desired rain to fall could also bring it in excess, and the result might well be catastrophic. Christianity invented the Devil to account for such disasters, but in ancient America fortune and misfortune were dealt out by the same gods. And those gods were of a difficult temper—like nature itself in the tropics, of whose changing moods they are the reflection.

Art in the Americas was not "free," as we understand that term. It had specific functions and duties. Which is why art for art's sake, in the European sense, was simply unknown in pre-Hispanic cultures, except for a few minor instances in the later period.

The artist was no more than a servant of society, and nameless. His work was all produced for religious purposes, either to be set up in the temples or to accompany the dead in their journey to the afterworld. The dead themselves served as intermediaries between the living and the gods. In ancient America, "art" was invented to lend emphasis to the prayers of the living. For such reasons, what the artist strove after was not, essentially, beauty, but an impression. Certainly it was not by chance that it was precisely in the period of Impressionist art in Europe that the artistic value of what these early cultures created came at last to be appreciated.

Aztecs, Incas, Mayas—their names resound like something out of a world of legend. And yet they were—they are—real. Their miraculous cultures are no more, yet their descendants live on today in the Upper Valley of Mexico, in the mountains and forests of Guatemala, on the high plateaus of Peru and Bolivia. But in the centuries since the Conquest, the Indian race has produced no really significant artist except for Rufino Tamayo. The anonymous artists who shaped grave offerings out of earth, the unknown sculptors who hewed images of the gods out of stone with no more than primitive tools, the nameless architects who erected mighty temples for the gods and palaces for their priests, all of them were bound to a wholly different world of belief than their descendants of today. Impenetrable as the past may seem, in many instances archaeologists have succeeded in finding their way to an understanding of the complex spirit of a world of forms which is so many-sided, fraught with so many contradictions.

Myths and prayers, sagas of the gods and legends of heroes—some were written down by the conquerors in the early colonial period, but before then they had been carved in stone or shaped from clay or recorded in a pictographic script, and they are the key to our comprehension of the thought of the ancient Indians. Four times, according to a Maya legend, the gods created man, the creature "who preserves and nourishes the gods."

In the face of a standing challenge from nature in the lands of hurricanes and volcanoes, the lands of great earthquakes, the lands where vast stretches of desert surround a few small isolated fertile river valleys, the Indians accomplished extraordinary things both technologically and artistically.

In the Upper Valley of Mexico, which acted as a kind of catch-basin for the streams of wild nomadic tribes that came down from the north, were found the first evidences of a great artistic past: the statuettes characterized by the name of the "pretty ladies" of Tlatilco. Here too stands what is probably the earliest architectural monument of America, Cuicuilco, "The-Place-of-Song-and-Dance," as well as the pyramid of Cholula, the world's largest in terms of inner area. Farther to the south was the region dominated by the Mixtecs and Zapotecs. The Mixtecs were masters in working clay and gold, while the Zapotecs were among the most grandiose architects of the New World. These peoples, each in their own way, made their own the stimuli that reached them from the Upper Valley of Mexico and from the Maya regions to the south.

By the time the first Europeans set foot on the ancient soil of the New World, most of the cities of the Maya civilization had long been covered over by the primeval forest. Only the very tallest of their buildings towered above the 200-foot-high jungle which had taken back as its own those terribly impressive ruins, mute witnesses of the city-states of that theocratic culture which, alone in either of the Americas, had developed a means of writing. But only about forty per cent of their hieroglyphics have been deciphered, and the larger part of them are still beyond our grasp. So even the most eloquent, the most communicative of the early cultures remains shrouded for us in a secret silence. Only the cities of postclassic Maya times on the Yucatan Peninsula have told us something of what happened to them: the priests of their jaguar cult left records of hurricanes and plagues, of grim wars between brother and brother, and at last of the slow death of a civilization which had once risen so high.

On the Isthmus of Panama were tribes which had taken refuge after having been driven out of their homes by stronger tribes. Their stone sculpture gives evidence of highly skilled craftsmanship, and their colorful and very imaginative ceramics still amaze us. That they left behind no architecture suggests that they never coalesced into any larger social organization, and that they were probably no more than small groups, each led by its own chieftain.

In Colombia the situation was quite different. There is every indication that the various tribes of that region would, in time, have united into a single kingdom had it not been for the Spanish Conquest.

It was in Peru, however, that a real empire was established, an empire even in our sense of the word. To speak, as has been done, of the "Socialist State of the Incas" is an exaggeration except as applied to the final century of a 3,000-year-old cultural development, but it could nevertheless boast of being the only great kingdom in the early Americas. The Aztecs in Mexico, likewise in the last century before the Spanish overran them, had subjugated at least two-thirds of all the Mexican tribes, but they never had the possibility, or perhaps the ambition, to weld the entire region into a single unified state. In Peru, religion may have played a great role in creating the centralized state. According to a widely diffused legend, the sun-god sent his four sons and daughters down to earth to found a kingdom. They were ordered to settle wherever their staves could penetrate easily the crust of the soil, and this occurred in the vicinity of Cuzco. The fact is, however, somewhat less fanciful: in the mid-thirteenth century, in this very isolated mountainous district, a ruling dynasty set itself up from among the Quechua tribe. As part of its policy, it gave a new impulse to the worship of the sun, the chieftain giving himself out to be born directly from the sun-god. Within something like a century, this small tribe in the Cuzco region managed to bring into being a "thousand-year empire" whose territory ranged over 350,000 square miles.

Artistic genius, however, lay in other hands—in those of the cultures which had come before the Incas, notably the Paracas and the Nazca. It was the potters of Moche and the goldsmiths of Chan Chan who possessed the real skill. The Incas, like the Aztecs, were latecomers, newly rich as it were, who simply appropriated what older cultures had achieved before them, and who thereby won the enmity of other peoples. This is the only way to explain how Hernando Cortés, with only 400 soldiers, and Francisco Pizarro, with less than 200, could have seized such great kingdoms: only rarely do we remember to take into account the many hundreds of thousands of auxiliary troops the foreign conquerors were able to recruit, without difficulty, from among the enemies of the Incas and the Aztecs.

LAND OF THE MAYAS
AND AZTECS

FROM THE RIO GRANDE TO EL SALVADOR

Just across the tawny canyon of the Rio Grande, to the south, everything is different. The sky is more intense, the clouds more restless. The soil is arid, the fields, like the people themselves, poorer. But children's laughter sounds brighter, happier, and the baying of the dogs is no more than a whimper.

The northern part of Mexico is mostly wasteland affording little means of subsistence to man. In pre-Hispanic times there was no important center of civilization in the north other than Casas Grandes. Just about at the level of the present capital, the mountainous wastes rise to a fertile basin, the Valley of Mexico, some 6,500 to 8,000 feet above sea level. Here the oldest American, the Tepexpan Man, was unearthed, and also the so-called "pretty ladies" of Tlatilco. Here too stands the oldest pyramid in Middle America, Cuicuilco, and the largest man-made structure in the world, the pyramid of Cholula. Farther to the south, in the upper valley of Oaxaca, there is the same geological formation, and this was the region inhabited by the Zapotecs and the Mixtecs. Still farther south, the Sierra Madre del Sur climbs even higher and then changes as it approaches present-day Guatemala. The Pacific side of this mountain range is infertile, and as yet scarcely studied by archaeologists. On the Atlantic side, the coastal area is largely a thirty-mile-wide strip of jungle, broadening out to the southeast and pushing into the stretch between the chalky plateau of the Yucatan Peninsula and the highlands of Guatemala. These lowlands of Tabasco, Chiapas, and the Petén were the seat of the most advanced early American civilization, that of the Mayas.

FROM THE RIO GRANDE TO EL SALVADOR – STYLES AND CULTURES

Time	Periods	Central Highland	Oaxaca	Northwest Mexico	Northern Gulf Coast	Central Gulf Coast	Southern Gulf Coast
1521			Beginning of the Spanish Conquest				
1400	Post-classic	Aztecs Chichimec	Aztec conquest Monte Albán V	Tarascans	Aztec conquest Pánuco VI	Aztec conquest	
1200	Post-classic	Culture Toltecs at Tula	(Mixtecs) Monte Albán IV	Toltec influence	Pánuco V	Cempoala (Totonacs)	
900		c. 900–1168	(Zapotecs) Monte Albán III B				
600	Classic	Teotihuacán IV	Tilantongo (Mixtecs) Monte Albán III A		Pánuco IV		Comalcalco (Maya)
300	Classic	Teotihuacán III Teotihuacán II	(Zapotecs) Monte Albán II	Nayarit Jalisco	Pánuco III	El Tajín	San Lorenzo
A.D. B.C.		Teotihuacán I	(Zapotecs) I	Colima	Pánuco II		Cerro de las Mesas Tres Zapotes
200	Experimental Age	Ticomán					
600	Experimental Age	Cuicuilco	Monte Albán I	Early Michoacán Chupícuaro	Pánuco I		
900		Tlapacoya Zacatenco	(La Venta influence)		(Huaxtecs)	Las Remojadas	La Venta (Olmecs)
1500		Tlatilco El Arbolillo	Monte Negro I (Mixtecs?)		Pavón		La Venta Culture
5000	Early planters	Chalco					
10000	Hunters and gatherers	Tepexpan Man					

U.S.A.

▲ Casas Grandes

RIO GRANDE

MEXICO

GULF OF MEXICO

Huaxtecs

● Tampico

▲ Tamuin

RIO PANUCO

NAYARIT

Tula ▲

Toltecs

Teotihuacán ▲

Tenochtitlán ▲

Aztecs

El Tajín ▲

Tarascans

JALISCO

▲ Chupícuaro

Tenayuca ▲

● Jalapa

Tlatilco ▲ ● Mexico D.F.

● Vera Cruz

▲ Tzintzuntzán

Puebla ● ▲ Cholula

Totonacs

COLIMA

Cuicuilco ▲

▲ Xochicalco

● Las Remojadas

MEZCALA

OAXACA

Tierra Blanca ▲

Mixtecs

Tres Zapotes ▲

Comalcalco ▲

Tilantongo ▲ ● Oaxaca

● La Venta

TABASCO

● San Lorenzo

USUMACINTA

M·AYA

▲ Monte Albán

▲ Mitla

Zapotecs

Palenque ●

CHIAPAS

Petén Maya

Bonampak ●

Piedras ▲ Uaxactún

San Cristóbal ▲ Negras ▲ Tikal

Las Casas

Yaxchilán ▲

Tayasal

● Comitán

▲ Chama

GUATEMALA

Highland Maya

Zaculeu ▲

Cobán ● Maya Quiriguá ▲

Izapa ▲

▲ Kaminaljuyú

● Guatemala

▲ Copán

HONDURAS

PACIFIC OCEAN

▲ El Baúl

▲ Tazumal

EL SALVADOR

Mérida ●

▲ Chichén Itzá

Mayapán ●

Uxmal ▲

Tulum ▲

Kabáh ▲ ● Cobá

● Cozumel

Sayil ●

Yucatán Maya

Survey of the most important sites

View from Monte Negro across
the Mixteca Alta. Oaxaca, Mexico.

It was modern Mexican artists like Diego Rivera and Miguel Covarrubias who were the first to appreciate the artistic importance of the so-called "pretty ladies" of Tlatilco. "Tlatilco," in the environs of Mexico City, means something like "The-Place-Where-Things-Lie-Hidden." In 1938, laborers in a brickworks came across these earliest evidences of Mexico's great artistic past. The age of these graceful clay figures is estimated by archaeologists at something between 2,500 and 3,000 years. They were offered to the dead to accompany them on their voyage to the other world, and at the interment they too underwent a ritual death by being broken into pieces.

Head of a girl. Whitish and red painted baked clay, height 5 1/2". Preclassic culture, c. 1300–700 B.C. From Tlatilco, Upper Valley of Mexico. Museo Nacional de Antropología, Mexico, D. F.

Seated woman. White and reddish painted baked clay, height 4". Preclassic culture, c. 1300–700 B.C. From Tlatilco, Upper Valley of Mexico. Museo Nacional de Antropología, Mexico, D. F. Collection Miguel Covarrubias.

Among the finds at Tlatilco were statues that strike one as modern. Many look as if they were produced by artists of our day. This figure of a woman with two faces, for instance, might be thought to be the prototype for Picasso's famous portrait of Dora Maar. Appearances, however, are deceiving. The great twentieth-century painter created his double-profile portrait between 1936 and 1938, but the first double-faced "pretty ladies" were not unearthed before 1940. It is still not clear if they were meant to be fertility-goddesses or merely dancers in the service of the shamans. It may be that, in this example, the artist doubled the head merely in an attempt to show it in movement, just as in the art of India, sculptors tried to show in simultaneity all the hand movements of the ritual dance of Shiva. But that, in any case, was more than 1,500 years later.

Female figure with double face. Baked clay, height 3²/₃″. Preclassic culture, c. 1300–700 B.C. From Tlatilco, Upper Valley of Mexico. Collection Dr. Kurt Stavenhagen, Mexico, D. F.

"Dancers." Red, yellow, and white painted baked clay, height $6^{1}/_{2}''$ and $6^{1}/_{8}''$. Preclassic culture, c. 1300–700 B.C. From Tlatilco, Upper Valley of Mexico. Private collection, Mexico, D. F.

The absence of male figures in this art, plus the great emphasis on bacchante-like female figures, suggests that they were made in a peaceful village society in which the religion which in later years came to dominate all aspects of life had not yet taken form. The excavations done in the 1950s by Mexican archaeologists turned up no trace of religious architecture in Tlatilco. In statuettes of the late period in this region, one finds facial features of a group from outside, the Olmecs, whom we shall meet again later in these pages.

The Tlatilco people lived on the maize, beans, and gourds they grew, rounding out this monotonous diet with game and fish. Ceramic vessels in the form of ducks (below) and fish, found in graves in Tlatilco, show fine observation of nature and testify to the craftsmanship and artistic ability of these early settlers in the Upper Valley of Mexico. Other sites of the same period have produced nothing of comparable quality. "The-Place-Where-Things-Lie-Hidden" was abandoned around the middle of the first millennium B.C. for reasons we do not know, though it may be that Lake Texcoco, which is now a dry basin, flooded over.

Duck. Baked clay, height 7 1/2″. Preclassic culture, c. 1300–700 B.C. From Tlatilco, Upper Valley of Mexico. André Emmerich Gallery, New York.

Painted clay figure, height 13 3/4″. Preclassic culture, c. 1500–1200 B.C. Chupícuaro style. From Chupícuaro, Michoacán, Mexico. Private collection, Los Angeles.

Besides Tlatilco, there are several hundred other settlements of the preclassic period known in Mexico and Central America. In all of them, in contrast to the subsequent classic period, there was profound veneration of Woman. Lacking in the Chupícuaro style is the subtle craftsmanship of the Tlatilco artists, but it has its own startling effectiveness in its characteristic ornamentation derived from woven patterns and in its strong coloring, achievements which, like the many experiments tried in other settlements, justify our calling this a formative period.

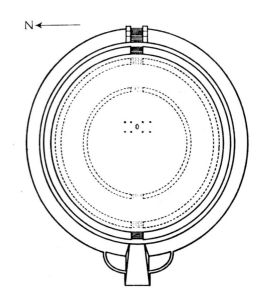

Clay shard, depicting a highly stylized man or demon, height 2³/₄″. Preclassic culture, c. 1000–600 B.C. From Cuicuilco, Valley of Mexico. Private collection, Munich.

Ground plan of the Pyramid of Cuicuilco, Upper Valley of Mexico.

Also in the environs of Mexico City is Cuicuilco, "The-Place-of-Song-and-Dance." Its round pyramid is the oldest religious construction in Mexico and Central America. The massive terrace, whose upper platform was reached by broad stairs, was some fifty-nine feet high and was crowned by an altar. It was probably between 300 and 400 B.C. that lava from the Xitli Volcano covered over the ancient sanctuary. Pottery from this region is coarse, peasantlike, powerful and monumental in form (above).

The "Mother Culture" of Mexico and Central America is how Miguel Covarrubias described the enigmatic civilization of the Olmecs who lived on the southern Gulf Coast and spread their religious and artistic ideas over a large part of these regions. Unmistakably symbolic is the squat, infantile type of human figure with protruding lips and broad nose found in small jade carvings (above) and in basalt monuments (see pages 20, 22). Often the mouth is shaped like a jaguar's, and archaeologists classify these figures as "Tiger-Face" and "Baby-Face."

Figure of "Baby-Face" type. Jade. Olmec Culture. c. 500 B.C.–A.D. 200. From La Venta, Tabasco, Mexico. Museo Nacional de Antropología, Mexico, D.F.

◀ The Pyramid of Cuicuilco, Upper Valley of Mexico. Preclassic culture, c. 1000–600 B.C.

Roughly around the time Tlatilco was abandoned and lava masses submerged the Pyramid of Cuicuilco, northern Central America was the scene of a deep-seated transformation. It is very likely that this sudden leap into a classic period was due to the diffusion of Olmec ideas and culture. Whether the Olmecs established their sway by military means or only through missionary work among more backward peoples is not known. It is certain, though, that traits of those unmistakable childlike faces made their way into the ceramics of Tlatilco and innumerable other local cultures, and that massive monuments were built in Olmec style far in the interior of present-day El Salvador (facing page). The word *olméca* is of Aztec origin, and its meaning is approximately "The-People-from-the-Land-of-Rubber," that is, the inhabitants of the southern Gulf Coast with its *chico zapote* trees which provide the raw material for chewing gum.

Here lay the home territory of the Olmecs, in La Venta, Tres Zapotes, and San Lorenzo Tenochtitlán. In 1940 Matthew Stirling, an authority on ancient America, found hidden in swampy mangrove forests a number of monumental heads of that culture, and the English sculptor Henry Moore later described them as the greatest works in spirit and form that he knew. In 1964 another of these colossal heads was found in San Lorenzo, the twelfth so far.

Colossal head. Basalt, height 5′ 3″. Olmec Culture, c. 500 B.C.–A.D. 200. Tres Zapotes, Vera Cruz, Mexico.

Warrior. Volcanic stone relief, height 5'. Olmec Culture,
c. 500 B.C.–A.D. 200. Tazumal, El Salvador.

Colossal head. Basalt, height 9'. Olmec Culture, c. 500 B.C.–A.D. 200. From San Lorenzo Tenochtitlán, Vera Cruz, Mexico. Museo Regional de Jalapa, Vera Cruz, Mexico.

The beginnings of the Olmec Culture—also called La Venta Culture after its chief site—are unknown. Wherever its artifacts turn up, they are in marked contrast to those of the preclassic period. The surprising stylistic discipline of Olmec art and its innovations in figurative form are evidence of a new religious conception and of a self-assured priestly class. The altar seen below shows a priest seated in a niche. On the bas-relief above him we recognize a highly stylized jaguar face. The great veneration of the jaguar and the development of a scientific calendar and a system of writing are among the most central achievements of Olmec culture. Their influence carried over to subsequent cultures and provided the basis of the remarkable calendar of the Maya as well as the point of departure for the highly important worship of the rain-god as it developed later. The earliest dates known for America were written on stone by the Olmecs: a stele from Tres Zapotes bears a date corresponding to September 2, 31 B.C. in our calendar.

Altar IV, front view. Basalt, height 5′ 4″. Olmec Culture, c. 500 B.C.–A.D. 200. From La Venta, Tabasco. Park Museum, Villa Hermosa, Tabasco, Mexico.

Figure lying prone. Basalt, dimensions of head 31 1/2 × 59″. Olmec Culture, c. 500 B.C.–A.D. 200. From Tres Zapotes, Vera Cruz. Market place of Tuxtla Santiago, Vera Cruz, Mexico.

If our only source of information were the tribal groups which came after them, we should know scarcely anything concrete about the Olmecs. But the Olmec artists, architects, and priests left us their own immense memorial. True, there is still much debate about what these monumental figures were meant to represent: gods, priests, princes, or merely the ideal of human beauty upheld by this culture? Not only their artistic mastery, but also the difficulties which had to be overcome in creating such gigantic statues for posterity, are impressive. The nearest stone quarry to La Venta lay something more than sixty-two miles away as the crow flies, that for San Lorenzo Tenochtitlán forty-six miles. Those centers and Tres Zapotes, from which came the statue seen above, were not cities in our sense but only religious centers with temple complexes and dwellings for priests, architects, and artists. But high dignitaries were also buried in these places (the archaeologist Stirling found almost 200 priceless jade figures in the grave of an official in La Venta). The people themselves lived scattered round about, near the fields they cultivated. They were held responsible for providing food for the priests as well as the gods, and only on festivals and market days did they themselves come in numbers to the sacred city.

The Olmecs were far and away the greatest sculptors of early America. The artistic quality of their jade carvings is no less than that of their monumental stone statues. Perhaps it is precisely the extremes which we find so fascinating in this Stone Age culture. Basalt is hard, jadeite and jade are even harder, and these were the favorite material of Olmec artists. Metal tools were unknown to this people, and their sculpture was carved with stone implements.

Acrobat. Steatite with traces of reddish paint, height 1 1/4″. Olmec Culture, c. 500 B.C.–A.D. 200. Provenance unknown. Collection Dr. Kurt Stavenhagen, Mexico, D. F.

Seated figure. Steatite with traces of red paint, height 9″. Olmec Culture, c. 500 B.C.–A.D. 200. From Teotitlán del Camino, Oaxaca, Mexico. Formerly Staatliches Museum für Völkerkunde, Berlin.

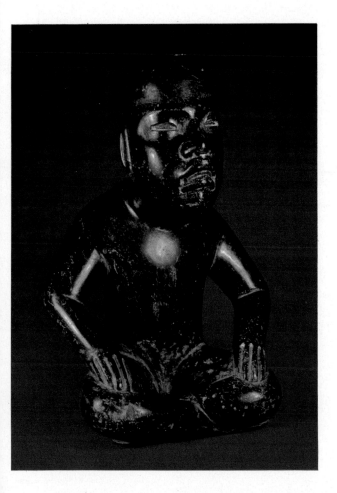

In the ceramics of the southern Gulf Coast, sensitively executed figures are in the minority. Most of the pieces lag far behind those of Tlatilco in quality. In architecture, too, there was nothing like the great achievements of the cultures which came later. With the disappearance of the Olmecs from the early American scene, the minor art of working in semiprecious stones was forgotten for centuries, and the major art of stone masonry was not destined to be revived until the coming of the Aztecs.

Despite an unmistakable uniformity in type, all the Olmec statues are quite diversified in physiognomy. This head in jadeite (right) has a deliberate deformation in the shape of the skull which was done for artistic reasons. Probably, as with other statues, it is a portrait of a priest-king. Where the Olmecs came from, who they were, where they finally went to—these are all unknown. What is certain, however, is that they laid the bases for the theocratic cultures which came after them, and that fundamental theological conceptions can be traced back to them.

◀ Ape looking toward heaven. Volcanic rock, height 45⅝″. Olmec Culture, c. 500 B.C.–A.D. 200. From La Venta Park Museum, Villa Hermosa, Tabasco, Mexico.

Head of a dignitary. Jadeite, height 8⅝″. Olmec Culture, c. 500 B.C.–A.D. 200. From Tenango del Valle, Oaxaca, Mexico. Museo Nacional de Antropología, Mexico, D. F.

Ceremonial ax. Green serpentine, height 8⅝". Mezcala style, c. 200 B.C.–A.D. 800. From the Mezcala region, Guerrero, Mexico. Collection Dr. Kurt Stavenhagen, Mexico, D. F. ▶

Ceremonial ax. Green serpentine, height 4¾". Mezcala style, c. 200 B.C.–A.D. 800. From the Mezcala region, Guerrero, Mexico. Collection Dr. Kurt Stavenhagen, Mexico, D. F.

The Mexican state of Guerrero is still unexplored territory for archaeologists. Systematic diggings have not been carried out in this mountainous country which is so difficult of access. Most of the objects we know were acquired from natives who had plundered the graves. The stylistically typical stone sculptures and masks come from the region to either side of the Mezcala River, whence the name given to the style. Completely characteristic of the style are the modern-looking ceremonial axes in the shape of starkly stylized human figures. In their extreme simplification, often verging on pure abstraction, every trace of humanity is shunned (facing page and below). The formalistic rigor of these figures, their withdrawn taciturnity, reveals nothing of the character of this cultural group, but they can be presumed to have been a highly warlike people. The lack of any distinctive architecture permits us to conclude that they never achieved any kind of union of larger social units under the leadership of a theocratic ruling class.

Seated effigy. Green serpentine, height 6 3/4 ″. Mezcala style, c. 200 B. C.–A. D. 800. From the Mezcala region, Guerrero, Mexico. Collection Dr. Kurt Stavenhagen, Mexico, D. F.

Teotihuacán was "by far the largest and most wonderful city of pre-Hispanic America, on a greater scale than Athens and larger than Rome"—this was the conclusion reached by one of the excavators of this ancient city, Jorge Acosta, who together with thirty-six other archaeologists and 550 laborers worked for many years to dig out the theocratic metropolis and restore its buildings. Acosta estimated the population at 250,000 inhabitants at the time the city reached its maximum growth, sometime between the third and fourth centuries of our era. The religious center alone covered an area of four and one-quarter square miles. From the outset, Teotihuacán was planned on a large scale, and must have been intended as a cultural, religious, economic, and political center. Such a metropolis guaranteed that there would be no splitting off into numerous small rival groups. All evidence suggests that the "golden age" of Mexico was a peaceful period. The immense pyramids and constructions, lying only thirty-one miles from Mexico's present-day capital, still bear evidence today of the vanished power of the priest-kings and the terrible fear of the gods that was instilled into their subjects.

View from the 213-foot-high Pyramid of the Sun across the Way of the Dead to the 147-foot-high Pyramid of the Moon. Classic Teotihuacán Culture, c. 100 B.C.–A.D. 400. Teotihuacán, Upper Valley of Mexico.

"They called the place Teotihuacán because it was the burial place of the kings, and the old men say that he who dies becomes a god. When it is said of someone that he is now *téotl* (god) it simply means that he is dead." This is what the Franciscan monk Sahagún wrote shortly after the Spanish Conquest, on the basis of what he had learned from his Aztec informants. In "That-Place-Where-They-Became-Gods," there was the ancient fire-god Xiutecuhtli (right) along with countless other divinities, all of whom were taken over by the succeeding cultures and only succumbed when Christianity was introduced in the sixteenth century.

Xiutecuhtli, the ancient fire-god. Volcanic stone, height 12". ▶
Teotihuacán Culture, c. 100 B.C.–A.D. 400. From Acatzingo, Puebla, Mexico. Museum für Völkerkunde, Vienna.

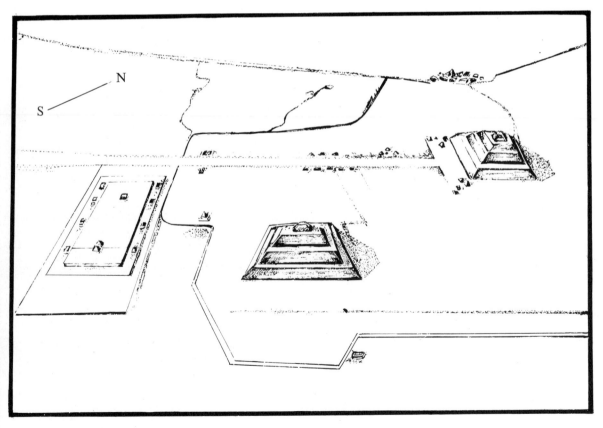

On the immensely broad stairway of the Pyramid of the Sun, before the eyes of the entire population, took place the awesome rites of the ancient religion. From the ground level, two widely separated flights of stairs mount to a landing where they combine into a single broad stairway, then they divide again and, after the highest terrace, once more come together. Severe and majestic as they course up the mighty pyramid, they symbolize a striving toward heaven, to the stars. Artistically, they infuse the architecturally static base of the pyramid with energy (below).

The Pyramid of the Sun. Height, c. 213′, length of side, 722′. Teotihuacán Culture, c. 100 B.C.–A.D. 400. Teotihuacán, Upper Valley of Mexico.

A surprising number of wall paintings have survived the destruction of the city. They were done in true fresco technique; as in the classic mural art of Italy, they were painted directly on a still damp layer of plaster "*al fresco*." Their subjects are the gods who appear in sumptuous garments and splendid headdresses and hold scrolls with hieroglyphic inscriptions along with shells and fertility symbols. The emotional impact of these frescoes is such that Cottie A. Burland was moved to describe them as "poems in fresco" (facing page).

Fresco with a rain-god. Detail, height c. 31″. Teotihuacán Culture,
c. 100 B.C.–A.D. 400. Teotihuacán, Upper Valley of Mexico.

The Pyramid of Quetzalcoatl. Teotihuacán Culture, c. 100 B.C.–A.D. 400. Teotihuacán, Upper Valley of Mexico.

Round bowl decorated with a figure of the rain-god Tlaloc. Earthenware, painted in so-called cloisonné technique, height 3″. Teotihuacán Culture. c. 100 B.C.–A.D. 400. Provenance unknown. Brooklyn Museum, New York.

The rain-god Tlaloc ("He-Who-Makes-Plants-to-Sprout") was, together with the water-goddess Chalchiutlicue ("The-Lady-with-the-Jade-Gown"), the most important divinity: on him depended the success or failure of the harvest. If the rains came too late, the crops withered. Tlaloc is especially often depicted in the art of ancient Mexico (above).

In ceramics of the classic period there is a clear distinction between pottery for daily use and a very much finer type made exclusively for religious purposes. The latter, usually painted in polychrome in a technique resembling cloisonné, with designs scratched or incised into a thin layer of stucco, are in both subject matter and technique small-scale relatives of the great mural paintings (see pages 33, 38). Even without any other evidence, the stylistic precision and deft execution of these fine ceramics would justify calling this a classic period.

"How great, however, was the mastery with which these people pinned down in their face masks—for all their simplification and stylization—the basic features of the Indian race which no camera can ever capture," wrote Sigvald Linné about these sculptures. Just what practical purpose the masks were meant to serve is not known. Possibly they had to do with burial rites for important persons; the burial customs of the ancient Peruvians of the coastal regions may give some clue to this: there, the dead were wrapped up like mummies and a "false head" was sewed on them. But it is more likely that they were pectoral ornaments worn by the priestly rulers. No such mask has ever been found *in situ;* all known examples were put on the market by grave looters who, for obvious reasons, are chary of revealing the sources of their finds.

Standing figure. Polished stone, height 6¹/₄". Teotihuacán Culture, c. 100 B.C.–A.D. 400. Provenance unknown. Collection Dr. Kurt Stavenhagen, Mexico, D. F.

Mask. Alabaster, height 7⁷/₈". Teotihuacán Culture, c. 100 B.C.–A.D. 400. Provenance unknown. Collection Dr. Kurt Stavenhagen, Mexico, D. F.

Head of a dignitary. Terra cotta, height $4^3/_4''$. Teoti- ▶
huacán Culture, c. 100 B.C.–A.D. 400. Provenance unknown. Museo Nacional de Antropología, Mexico, D. F.
Miguel Covarrubias Collection.

Vase. Earthenware painted in so-called cloisonné tech-
nique, height c. $9^7/_8''$. Teotihuacán Culture, c. 100 B.C.–
A.D. 400. From Teotihuacán, Upper Valley of Mexico.
Museo Nacional de Antropología, Mexico, D. F.

The esoteric expressive style of the masks and
clay figures (above) contrasts with another
style which is virtually abstract and was used
chiefly for frescoes and pottery decoration
(left). On the vase seen here, the principal
subject is the rain-god Tlaloc, but his
image is reduced to an abstract geometrical
formula. The artist, or the priest from whom
he took his orders, aimed clearly to separate
the invisible and divine from everything
visible and human. This effect of alienation,
of divine remoteness, is found again, and
not without reason, in the Tiahuanaco Culture of the southern Peruvian highlands (see
pages 194–98).

Mask of the bat-god. Pieces of jade inlaid with shell, height 11 1/8". Zapotec Culture, Monte Albán II style, c. 200 B.C.–A.D. 200. From Monte Albán, Oaxaca. Museo Nacional de Antropología, Mexico, D. F.

"I could learn nothing which seemed to have any semblance of truth about the earliest appearance of this people, nor about the origins of their rulers. . . . To make themselves seem more formidable, they all pretend to be sons of jaguars and other savage beasts. The great leaders of ancient family claim to be offshoots of primevally old, huge shade trees, and those who glory in their own invincibility and steadfastness pretend that they were born from crags and cliffs." That was all that the Spanish chronicler Burgoa could glean, at the start of the sixteenth century, about the origins of the Zapotecs. Four hundred years later, we have not got much further in solving the enigma. In the ancient Zapotec settlements have been found images of their gods with attributes of the jaguar and bat (above).

The Zapotec Culture spread out geographically more or less between the two great theocratic power blocs, that of Teotihuacán to the northwest and that of the Mayas to the southeast. On a mountain they themselves had leveled off, Monte Albán ("White Mountain"), which overlooks three valleys, the Zapotecs laid out a temple enclosure which is both awesome in its proportions and architecturally daring. For more than 2,000 years, during which it was repeatedly enlarged and added to, this was the religious center for the Zapotecs. In contrast to the builders of La Venta and Teotihuacán, who merged with other tribal groups, the Zapotecs, like the Mayas who were their neighbors to the southeast, have remained until our times a closed tribal unit which has even clung to its ancient language. The first epoch in Monte Albán's history was obviously strongly influenced by the Olmecs. Almost life-size figures full of rhythm and movement were carved in low relief out of smoothed-down stone surfaces (see page 44). Some of these *Danzantes* ("Dancers") are accompanied by pictographs which undoubtedly stand for dates and tell us that, long before the high point of Greek civilization, the builders of Monte Albán were already devising a calendar. In the pottery of the Monte Albán I Culture, which goes back to 1500 B.C., there are also typical Olmec traits such as the jaguar mouth from which was to develop later the snarling mouth of the rain-god (see page 42). It was not until the tenth century of our era that Monte Albán was abandoned. Probably it was the Mixtecs who drove the Zapotecs from their sacred

mountain, because after that date the conquerors used it as a burial ground for their kings. In 1932 vast treasures of gold and precious stones which proved to be grave offerings of Mixtec origin were found in Tomb 7 of the Zapotec sanctuary.

The Zapotecs were a race of great builders who worked out the total ensemble as well as minor details on the basis of a ground plan, conceived the definitive form of the open square, and integrated their entire conception into the surrounding landscape. The difference between European and early American ways of building is nowhere more obvious than at Monte Albán. Here stands a completely isolated sanctuary which is not hemmed in and cluttered by any nonreligious architecture. No humble dwellings cluster around a cathedral as in the European Middle Ages, no patrician palaces rub shoulders with temples in a false show of familiarity as in ancient Rome.

The sanctuary of Monte Albán. Zapotec Culture, c. 600 B.C.–A.D. 900. Monte Albán, Oaxaca, Mexico.

Incense burner. Baked clay, height 6⅝″. Olmec-influenced style, Monte Albán I Culture, c. 800–200 B.C. From Oaxaca, Mexico. Private collection, Munich.

As in Teotihuacán, so too in Monte Albán the north-south axis is not adhered to strictly in the layout of the city, and this can undoubtedly be traced back to the orientation of the stars. Originally there were only a few buildings on scattered hilltops. With the centuries, the mountain top was razed to a level and transformed into an immense flat terrain. At both the north and south ends, the vast quadrangle, which is almost 2,300 feet long and 820 feet wide, is framed by the largest of the groups of buildings. The temple on the northern side, seen here, rises above a platform not much under 60,000 square yards in area, and its 141-foot-wide staircase, the broadest in early America, flows down harmoniously into the open place. Once, twelve columns built of rough-hewn rock supported the roof of the gallery. Through the disposition of its buildings, the sanctuary of Monte Albán resembled a tremendous amphitheater, but it differed from those of Greek and Roman antiquity in two respects: for one, its plan was oblong, and for the other, the religious spectacle of its sumptuously dressed priests took place on the staircase and platforms while the spectators were massed in the open quadrangle below. The Zapotecs were not partial to smooth stucco façades such as had been developed to such perfection in Teotihuacán. The platforms and staircases of their pyramids were built out of rough-hewn stones and sun-dried clay—after all, as the Spanish chronicler Burgoa reported, were not their ancestors "born from crags and cliffs"?

The 141-foot-wide staircase of the northern temple. Zapotec Culture, built between the fifth and sixth centuries. Monte Albán, Oaxaca, Mexico.

Something like a thousand years lie between the bas-reliefs the first inhabitants of Monte Albán left behind (above) and the burial urns made in the classic period of Zapotec Culture (facing page). We simply do not know exactly what these strange figured vessels were used for: despite appearances, they are in fact vessels; behind the figure is a cylindrical receptacle. Of the many urns that have been found in the antechambers of tombs or in the graves themselves, all have been empty. As for the personage depicted, the rich garments, exuberant headdress made to resemble animal fur and exotic bird feathers, and the profusion of jeweled ornaments, all suggest, if not a god himself, at least a high priest. These sensitively executed figures never venture so far as complete realism. They are always subject to a certain strictly patterned norm of rhythm and symmetry,

Two so-called *Danzantes* (Dancers), the left-hand one with a hieroglyphic inscription. Stone reliefs, height c. 4′ 8″. Olmec-influenced style, Monte Albán I, c. 800–200 B.C. Monte Albán, Oaxaca, Mexico.

Figure urn. Terra cotta, height 25⅝″. Zapotec Culture, Monte Albán III, c. A.D. 250–700. From Oaxaca, Mexico. Collection Señora Machida Armila, Mexico, D. F.

not the least in their elaborate ornamental accessories which, technically, could only have been formed out of special clay found in Oaxaca and baked with a much improved technique. In pose and facial expression, many of the figures suggest an inner calm, a resignation before a future already dark in portent. Neither frank laughter nor any grimace, no expression of either joy or grief is to be found in these art works which accompanied the dead into the underworld. Because of its wealth, as revealed in its splendid finery and ornaments, the Upper Valley of Oaxaca was never to know peace. Mixtecs, Aztecs, and finally the Spaniards all coveted it. Cortés, the conqueror of Mexico, knew what he was about when he requested from the Spanish throne the Upper Valley of Oaxaca as his personal fief.

Figured urn depicting a musician. Earthenware, height 17³/₄″. Zapotec Culture, Monte Albán III-A style, c. A.D. 250–700. From San Pedro Martín, Oaxaca. Collection Howard Leigh, Mitla, Oaxaca, Mexico.

Nothing of the poetry of the classic period has come down to us, and only a few clues as to its music. Among the latter are depictions of musicians (facing page) from which we can learn something about the instruments used. To set the rhythm, tortoise shells were employed. There were also bells which were worn by the dancers (below). In the classic period the bells were made of clay, and it was not until the fourteenth century that they were cast in copper. Rattles made from gourds were also used to mark the rhythm, and for melodic instruments there were conch shells as well as trumpets, flutes, and fifes made of earthenware. Stringed instruments, so prominent in the Old World, were unknown to the Indians. We know that the children in the state schools (*calmecac*) of the Aztecs had the task of performing music and the "songs of the gods." The special deity for music and dance was Macuilxochitl ("Five-Flowers"), along with Xochipilli, who was known as the "Flower-Prince."

Dancer with bells on his ankles. Earthenware, height 2²/₃″. Zapotec-Mixtec Mixed Culture. c. 1200–1400. From Mixtuatlán, Oaxaca. Museo Frissell, Mitla, Oaxaca, Mexico.

Standing dignitary. Terra cotta, height 24³/₈". Olmec-influenced early Zapotec Culture, Monte Albán II style, c. 200 B.C.–A.D. 200. From Monte Albán, Oaxaca. Museo Nacional de Antropología, Mexico, D. F.

Façade of the palace at Mitla. Zapotec-Mixtec Mixed ▶ Culture, c. 1200–1400. Mitla, Oaxaca, Mexico.

Mitla is the best-preserved ruined city of Pre-Columbian Mexico. The fact that its builders made no effort to copy the great religious center of Monte Albán tells us much about their architectural skill. Here, indeed, architecture leaped several steps ahead. At Monte Albán, the rough-hewn stone columns serve only as mono-lithic weight-bearing supports, and the façades are crudely rugged. In Mitla, the façade was transformed into a subtle, infinitely complex play of geometrical forms which seems to have overlooked no possible variation. The jigsaw puzzle that results is dramatic and lends a note of vitality to the dead city—Mitla's original name was Mictlán, the "Entrance-into-the-Kingdom-of-Death" (facing page).

Today there are still islets of Mixtec speech within the regions settled by the Zapotecs. This bears out the observations of the Spanish chroniclers that those two groups intermingled in part through intermarriage, in part through the warlike incursions of the Mixtecs into Zapotec territory. Probably Mitla belonged initially to the Zapotecs and at least once later changed hands. Only fragments of frescoes survive, but they are in the style of Mixtec picture-writing and tell us that this gifted tribe of farmers from the mountains lived, for a time at least, in Mitla.

The palace at Mitla. Zapotec-Mixtec Mixed Culture, c. 1200–1400. Mitla, Oaxaca, Mexico.

With the Mixtecs, who prepared the way for Aztec art and science, we have reached historical times. Their pictographic writings painted on buckskin (see page 55) trace the genealogies of the leading ruling families back to the year 692. The Mixtecs were admired for their colored pottery, extraordinary bone carvings, and, not least, for their goldsmith work, and all these wares were eagerly sought after. But it was precisely their artistic skills which led to their downfall. In 1494, after innumerable battles across the years, the Aztecs finally overcame the Mixtecs and dragged away their highly proficient craftsmen to work in the conquerors' capital.

Clay shard, $2^1/_4 \times 2^1/_4$". Mixtec Culture, c. 900–1494. From Mixteca Alta, Oaxaca, Mexico. Private collection, Munich.

Tripod bowl. Earthenware, height c. $4^3/_4$". Mixtec Culture, c. 900–1494. From Oaxaca. Museo Nacional de Antropología, Mexico, D. F.

Bowl with a god painted on its body. Earthenware, height 7″. Mixtec Culture, c. 900–1494. From Mixteca Alta, Oaxaca. Museo Regional, Oaxaca, Mexico.

In all of Mexico, nothing surpasses the richly decorated pottery of the Mixtecs. Uniquely characteristic of their work are the three-legged spherical cups and bowls. Almost always the feet are formed into jaguar claws or eagle heads. In glowing colors made brighter by polishing, gods or historical personages are painted on them in the style of the Mixtec pictorial writing (above). Some vessels are decorated with geometrical ornaments like those on the façades at Mitla or with severely stylized motifs such as the "Plumed Serpent," a combination of animal and human attributes. This unique type of pottery was developed relatively late, certainly not before 1300, and was still in use when the Spaniards seized the country.

Human skull inlaid with pieces of turquoise and shell. Height c. $7^1/_8''$. Mixtec Culture, c. 900–1494. From Monte Albán, Oaxaca. Museo Regional, Oaxaca, Mexico.

Monte Negro—the "Black Mountain"—which lies above Tilantongo in the Mixteca Alta Mountains, was the seat of the oldest ruling group of Mixtecs. Its early pottery (Monte Negro I style) can be dated in the first millennium B.C., but it too reveals certain elements of Olmec style. In the Codex Vindobonensis (facing page) the founder of the capital is said to be the chieftain 4-Alligator. The Codex Teozacoalco speaks of the birth of Princess 7-Flower which, by our reckoning, took place in the year 692. It was then that the Tilantongo dynasty began; as we know from other sources, it continued its sway until 1580, at which time the Mixtec chieftain was baptized by the Spaniards with the name Francisco de Mendoza.

The ruins of Monte Negro above Tilantongo, Oaxaca, Mexico. Mixtec Culture, c. 900–1494.

Most Pre-Columbian pictographic writing that has survived comes from the area under Mixtec cultural influence. The Codex Vindobonensis was brought to Europe as a gift for King Manoel of Portugal. The king died in 1521, so it seems likely that this folding book was one of the two mentioned by Cortés. Probably it came from a temple on the Gulf Coast, a region inhabited by the Mixtecs and still called Mixtequilla. The book consists of a long strip of buckskin made up of several smaller pieces joined together and folded in such a way as to form fifty-two pages. The painter must have lived around 1350, since that is the latest date in his history of the Mixtecs. The introduction of the book goes back to Genesis, as it were, with an account of the gods and the mythical birth of the four founders of the Mixtec people. In addition, the most important duties and directives of the priesthood are expounded. At the upper left of the page reproduced here, Quetzalcoatl-9-Wind separates the heavens from the waters. Below, in the middle, the rain-god Tlaloc is depicted as a mountain, probably a symbol for Mixteca Alta, since the inhabitants of that mountainous region were designated by their neighbors as "Those-of-the-Cloud-Land, Those-of-the-Rain-Land."

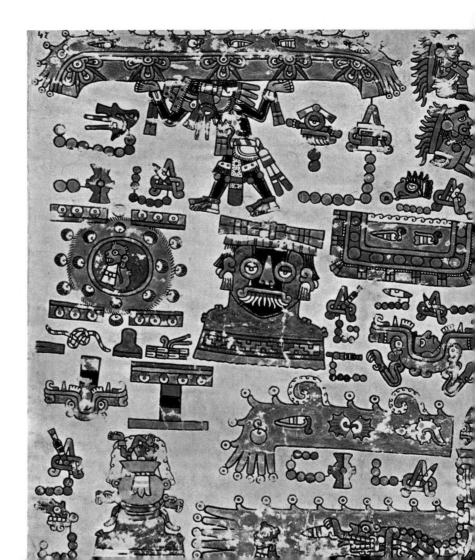

Left half of page 47 of the Codex Vindobonensis. 8⁵/₈ × 7¹/₂″. Mixtec Culture, c. 1350. From central Gulf Coast (?), Mexico.

Ritual drinking vessel. Greenish serpentine, *chalchihuite*, height 14⁵/₈″. Mixtec Culture, c. 900–1494. Provenance unknown. Museum für Völkerkunde, Vienna.

Mask of the god of spring Xipe Totec, "Our-Lord-Who-Was-Flayed." Gold, cast by the "lost-wax" method, height about 2³/₄". Mixtec Culture. c. 900–1494. From Monte Albán, Tomb 7, Oaxaca. Museo Regional, Oaxaca, Mexico.

The cylindrical vessel in the shape of a god's head (facing page) also has on it a great many mythological figures and symbols in bas-relief, and was probably used in rituals. It is a rare example of Mixtec stonework, since that people made much less use of stone than did their later adversaries, the Aztecs. The real specialty of the Mixtecs was goldsmith work. Their homeland, the Mixteca Alta massif, lies near the old roads which linked the northern and southern continents. Thus it was not by chance that this was a promising terrain for metalwork, an art which probably spread from the Andean cultures in Peru and Bolivia by way of Colombia and Panama. Mixtec gold ornaments often look like filigree work but were, in fact, done by the so-called lost-wax method of casting. "Like something in dreams, and yet made by the hands of men," is the way Bartolomé de Las Casas, Bishop of Chiapas, missionary, and defender of the Indians, described the Mixtec jewelry, of which only a small portion escaped being melted down in the crucibles of the European conquerors (above).

The subtropical region of the central Gulf Coast was the homeland of the Tajín Culture. It is not certain if the Totonacs, the present inhabitants of that area, are descendants of the people who gave rise to that culture. In marked contrast to the Mixtecs, the Tajín people were a peaceful folk dressed neatly in white and who delighted in song and dance. Their temple architecture and their sculpture in clay or stone have a kind of baroque charm absent from the art of the highland peoples. Among their deities there was even a god who laughed, the only one in the awesome pantheon of pre-Hispanic Mexico. From the standpoint of art history, the culture of the central Gulf Coast, known also as Totonac, is a unique phenomenon: its pottery has Maya-like traits, its sculpture in the later period was influenced by the Toltecs, and its methods of building owed nothing to any other people.

Reclining figure. Yellow-brown stone, 6^1/$_2$ × 16^1/$_2$″. Culture of the central Gulf Coast (Tajín Culture), c. 500–1200. Provenance unknown. The Cleveland Museum of Art, Cleveland.

Standing figure. Baked clay, height 12¹/₄″. Culture of the Gulf Coast, c. 500–1400.
From El Faisán, Vera Cruz. Museo Regional de Jalapa, Vera Cruz, Mexico.

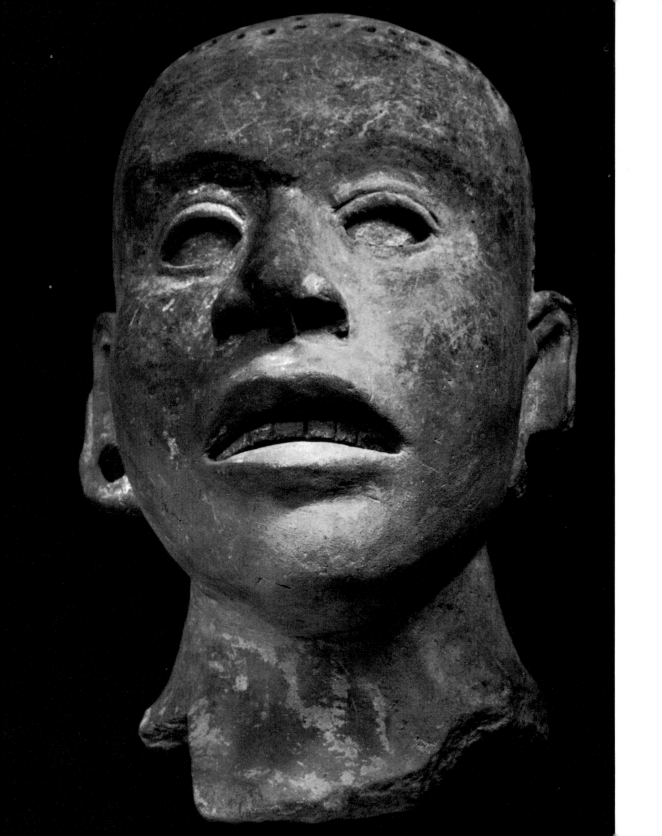

Fragment of a male head. Baked clay, height 10¹/₄". Culture of the central Gulf Coast, c. 500–1200. From Ignacio de la Llave, Vera Cruz. Museo Regional de Jalapa, Vera Cruz, Mexico.

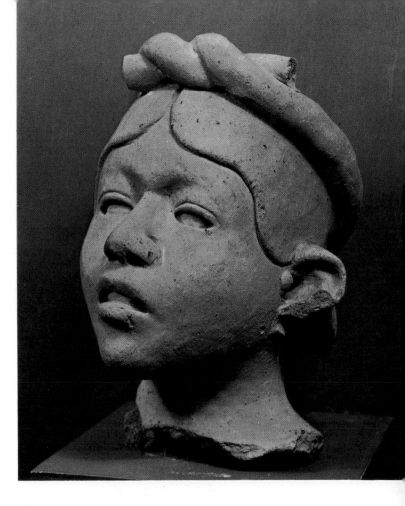

Head of a girl. Baked clay, height 3¹/₂". Culture of the central Gulf Coast, c. 500–1200. Provenance unknown. Museo Regional de Jalapa, Vera Cruz, Mexico.

"More human than divine" is how one writer described these subtle terra cottas of the Mexican Gulf Coast. From them we learn much about the way this ancient people dressed. The figures among their grave offerings are not lacking in jewelry such as necklaces and earplugs, in carefully arranged hairdresses, and, in many cases, in facial painting. Many of the styles of clothing they wore have persisted through the ages: the twisted head-kerchief on the young girl seen here (above) is still worn by many Mexican women. Another distinction of these terra cottas is their portraitlike character, something never achieved by artists in other regions and most probably never even attempted. Almost all the sculpted pieces show a physical type quite unlike that of the highland Indians, tending a little to fleshiness, at least in older persons. As against the fanatical picture of the world held by the highlanders, these people had a somewhat more Dionysiac conception of life. In the lowest strata of diggings on the Gulf Coast are found once again the childlike faces of the Olmecs, and in the upper strata polychrome pottery which, in both form and decoration, reveals Mixtec influence. Between these, however, are found objects that re-create for us the human aspects of a distinct and separate culture which takes its name either from a ruin (El Tajín) or from a great archaeological site (Las Remojadas).

Only minor traces of the original painting on sculpted figures have been able to withstand the ravages of a subtropical climate. An exception, however, is the bitumen paint used to accentuate details such as the pupils of the eyes and also, often, the facial decorations which, no doubt, were a sign of the social position and importance of the persons portrayed. The head shown at the right bears on its cheeks the calendar sign "*olin*," which means the revolution or movement of time, a hieroglyph which, in the Aztec period, symbolized the sun-god.

Head of a man, probably the sun-god. Baked clay, height 9″. Culture of the central Gulf Coast, c. 500–1200. Provenance unknown. Collection Dr. Kurt Stavenhagen, Mexico, D. F.

Vase in the form of a human figure with arm raised in greeting. Alabaster, height 8¼″. Culture of the central Gulf Coast, c. 500–1450, probably under Mixtec influence. Provenance unknown. Brooklyn Museum, New York.

Seated dignitary. Baked clay,
height c. 5¹/₈″. Culture of the
central Gulf Coast, c. 500–1200.
From Tierra Blanca region,
Vera Cruz. Collection Dr. Kurt
Stavenhagen, Mexico, D. F.

Fragment of a jaguar head. Baked clay with bitumen painting, height 7^1/$_2$″. Culture of the central Gulf Coast, c. 500–1200. From Tlahuac, Vera Cruz. Collection Stendahl, Los Angeles.

On the Gulf Coast also, the jaguar remained the most feared beast. In contrast to the preceding Olmec Culture, however, which saw the jaguar as a demon, the later depictions conceived the animal in realistic fashion, and they testify to the artists' profound powers of observation. The nostrils, sharp teeth, and watchful eyes are handled in a masterful manner. Nothing is dramatized. Unfortunately, the body of this statue could not be found, probably because it was smashed ritually before it was laid away with the dead.

Palma in the form of a bird. Basalt, height about 15³/₄″. Culture of the central Gulf Coast, c. 500–1200. Provenance unknown. Collection Dr. Kurt Stavenhagen, Mexico, D. F.

An entirely distinct form, native only to the Gulf Coast, is known as the *palma* because of its resemblance in shape to a palm frond. What purpose these sculptures served is not yet known precisely, though they may have been a replica in stone of a ballplayer's insignia of rank, or perhaps merely a kind of architectural ornament. All that is certain is that their external form—like that of the *yugo* (yoke) and the *hacha* (ax) —was immutable, and that the artist had to conform to it, whatever his fancy might suggest. With what mastery this was done can be seen in this depiction of a sea bird.

Fragment of a head, the so-called *Caras Sonrientes* type ("Smiling Faces"). Baked clay, height $5^2/_3$". Culture of the central Gulf Coast, c. 500–1200. Provenance unknown. Collection Dr. Kurt Stavenhagen, Mexico, D. F.

Water bird. Baked clay with traces of white painting, legs added in restoration, length c. $29^1/_2$". Culture of the central Gulf Coast, c. 500–1200. Provenance unknown. Collection Dr. Kurt Stavenhagen, Mexico, D. F.

Unique in their human quality are certain figures with a radiant smile, the so-called *Caras Sonrientes*, the "Smiling Faces." In outward appearance they resemble Asiatic gods more than those of pre-Hispanic Mexico. Perhaps they are images of ritual dancers, whose inviting gestures and air of radiant benevolence contrast markedly with what we are familiar with in other theocratic societies. More probably they may represent the pulque-god, the god of drunken ecstasy native to the Gulf Coast, or his priests. In the highly realistic art of this region are also found many depictions of animals. It is not known if these are simply expressions of the artists' fancy or images symbolizing mythical concepts associated with animals. The water bird seen below has a strong formal resemblance to Egyptian depictions of the ibis.

El Tajín ("The Lightning," in Totonac) was the name given on the Gulf Coast to the rain-god as well as to the ruins of the ancient sacred city in that region, apparently the only one in all of Mexico to survive the collapse of the theocratic culture of the classic period. From diggings in this site deep in the jungle, we know that it was abandoned sometime between 1130 and 1180, but do not yet know why. The most prominent edifice in the city is the seven-tiered Pyramid of the 365 Niches. The unmistakable, individualistic style was not taken up in other regions. Its combination of geometrical rigor and baroque richness makes it seem almost un-Mexican.

Perhaps originally there may have been an idol in each of the 365 niches, one for each of the gods who governed a day of the year. On the other hand, these windowlike apertures may have had no practical purpose and been merely decorative, like the nonfunctional flights of steps which also are typical of Tajín architecture. It was by ladders, not stairs, that the separate ledges or inner rooms were reached. The massive, projecting staircases constitute an extraordinary masterwork—a masterwork of the impractical. Nonetheless, the builders did not lack for practical know-how, as is shown by the way they roofed over the inner chambers. The ceilings were constructed with a light cement made of grated mussel shells and pumice stone combined with wood and plant fibers, a technical innovation which did not spread beyond this small area of the central Gulf Coast.

The Pyramid of the 365 Niches at El Tajín. Height 59′. Culture of the central Gulf Coast, c. 500–1200. El Tajín, Vera Cruz, Mexico.

On the Gulf Coast as elsewhere, ceramics are the best medium for tracing art and society back to their remote past. At first, along with strikingly ugly statues of an unknown fertility-goddess, there were male "Remojadas" figures. For centuries they followed stereotyped models, and it is moving to observe how, little by little, out of the unformed mass of clay there began to appear three-dimensional, sensitive sculpture. These small burial statuettes are not lacking in such details as decorative ornaments, necklaces, and earplugs, or even carefully arranged coiffures. Bitumen pigment was already used on the face in very early times, and this is typical of the art of this region. Only relatively late, certainly not before the ninth century, did there appear the markedly human traits which strongly resemble the physiognomy we find in classic Maya art. This comparison is particularly valid for the subtle modeling of the mouth area and for the inward-turning gaze.

Fragment of a head. Terra cotta, height 6½". Culture of the central Gulf Coast, c. 500–1200. Provenance unknown. Collection Dr. Kurt Stavenhagen, Mexico, D. F.

Ground plan and schematic diagram of a side view of the Pyramid of the 365 Niches in El Tajín, Vera Cruz, Mexico. Culture of the central Gulf Coast (Tajín Culture), c. 500–1200.

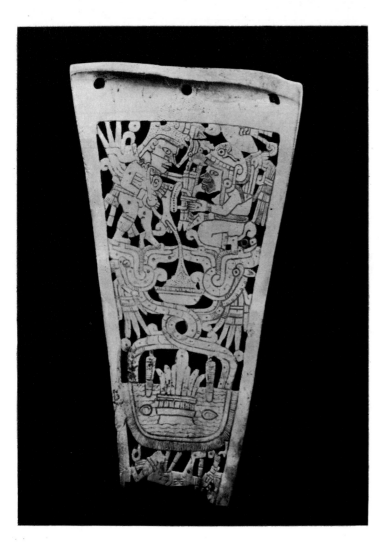

Ornamental pendant. Shell, height $3^7/_8$". Huaxtec Culture (Pánuco V), c. 1000–1250. From region of the present-day city of Vera Cruz. Middle American Research Institute, Tulane University, New Orleans.

The Huaxtecs, the Aztecs insisted, were drunkards and magicians. These northeastern neighbors of the Totonacs have constituted an independent tribal entity for almost 3,000 years. Only shortly before the Spanish Conquest did they finally become a tributary of the Aztecs. The highly independent Huaxtecs, whose descendants still inhabit the northern Gulf Coast, are of Maya stock. In the first millennium B.C. they broke away from the other Mayas and took no part in the great cultural progress of that group. Among the Maya achievements they never profited from were the pictographic script and the so-called false arch (the corbeled vault) in architecture. But their craftsmen found their own style. Especially valued were their cutout decorative pendants. The one above is incised with two gods performing some ritual act.

Vase with painted face. Earthenware, height $5\frac{1}{8}''$. Culture of northern Mexico, Casas Grandes style, c. 1300–1500. From Casas Grandes, Chihuahua, Mexico. Museo Nacional de Antropología, Mexico, D. F.

The culture of Casas Grandes ("The Great Houses") is a link between the Mexican and North American cultures. This ceramic pot was unearthed in the Casas Grandes site, near the United States border. In both form and coloring it is closer to the art of the New Mexico and Arizona Indians (Hohokám and Anasazi) than to that of its neighbors to the south. The diggings show that Casas Grandes was a peaceful agricultural village community without any strict social organization.

The ceramic ware of the Northwestern Coast seems like a belated offshoot of the preclassic period. Until recently it was thought that the creators of this anecdotal art were the Tarascans, the tribe still inhabiting this region. However, the Tarascans possess a saga of their wanderings similar to that of the Aztecs, and from it can be deduced that they immigrated into this region only relatively late. We are left, then, as so often in archaeology, with no more than the present-day names of the states of Colima, Nayarit, and Jalisco to categorize these small but very expressive grave offerings. The theocratic cultures, in their terra cottas, were restricted to depictions of the pantheon of their gods and to memorials of their sacred princes. Here, on the Northwestern Coast, we are offered, however, a veritable Human Comedy. The unrelenting immobility of theocratic art was not welcomed here, nor was there any willingness to allow the austere notions of their southern neighbors, with their sacred city of Teotihuacán, to infiltrate this happier region. The ceramics native to these parts were not burdened with religious obsessions. Instead, they portray the daily round of men's lives. Often they are downright comic, sometimes verging on caricature, or they may be simply uncouth and, not rarely, openly profane. Indeed, many of the objects dug up in this region seem, to our eyes, strikingly modern.

Standing male figure. Terra cotta, height 23⅝". Nayarit style, Northwestern Coast Culture, c. 300–1000. From Nayarit, Mexico. Formerly Galerie Wels, Salzburg.

Nowhere else in either of the Americas was the subject of mother and child so often treated as here on the Northwestern Coast of Mexico. The anonymous sculptor of this piece gave a picture of the experience of motherhood which is partly sentimental, partly shattering in its expressive intensity. We owe the rich treasury of these statues, which are highly prized by both private collectors and museums, to the local custom of burying the dead in very deep shaft graves and of not "putting to death" the grave offerings by breaking them.

Seated mother and child. Terra cotta, height 5^1/$_2$″. Colima style, culture of the Northwestern Coast, c. 300–1000. From Colima, Mexico. Collection Dr. Kurt Stavenhagen, Mexico, D.F.

Seated figure. Terra cotta, height 6⁷/₈″. Colima style, culture of the Northwestern Coast, c. 300–1000. From Colima, Mexico. Collection Dr. Kurt Stavenhagen, Mexico, D. F.

Seated maiden. Terra cotta, height 11³/₈″. Colima style, culture of the Northwestern Coast, c. 300–1000. From Colima, Mexico. Dr. Kurt Stavenhagen, Mexico, D. F.

Colima ceramics are livelier and more three-dimensional than those of the nearby state of Nayarit. They avoid anything static, and their entire conception is basically different. Many of the figures, like the one to the right, seem so modern as to recall, in their construction and form, a statue such as Maillol's *La Nuit*.

Musician with a conch shell as wind instrument. Red-painted terra cotta, height 15″. Colima style, culture of the Northwestern Coast, c. 300–1000. From Colima, Mexico. Collection Stendahl, Los Angeles.

A favorite subject of artists on the Northwestern Coast, and one of the few with a religious background, was dogs (below). As with many ancient peoples, dogs were thought to accompany the dead on their journey. Shortly after the Mexican Conquest, the Franciscan monk Sahagún explained: "It is said that, as companion, he (the dead man) had a small dog, a yellow one wearing a skein of loose cotton yarn as collar. It is said that the dog carries the dead man across the nine-fold stream to Mictlán. . . . There the stream is wide, and dogs are the ferrymen, so that when one of them recognizes its master it leaps into the water to convey him across. That is why the natives breed so many dogs, for it is said that neither white nor black dogs can pass over into the land of the dead. It is said that white dogs protest, 'I have already washed myself,' and black ones, 'I have just painted myself black.' Only the yellow dog can cross the river." The color of the dog is, therefore, related to his specific divine function: in the Aztec religion, yellow was the color of the death-god.

Standing female nude. Terra cotta, height 6⁷/₈″. Early Colima style, culture of the Northwestern Coast, c. 100 B.C.–A.D. 500. From Colima, Mexico. Private collection, Munich.

Dog. Terra cotta, height 4¹/₂″. Colima style, culture of the Northwestern Coast, c. 300–1000. From Colima, Mexico. Private collection, Munich.

Warrior with spear. Terra cotta, height 14$^{1}/_{8}$". Nayarit style, culture of the Northwestern Coast, c. 300–1000. From the Ixtlán del Río region, Nayarit, Mexico. Collection Stendahl, Los Angeles.

In contrast to the ceramics of Colima and Jalisco (page 80), those of Nayarit often seem comic and grotesque. As everywhere on the Northwestern Coast, here too the subject matter is drawn chiefly from everyday life: mothers and children, the healthy and the ill, warriors, ballplayers. One seeks in vain for depictions of specific gods. Among the peculiarities of this culture is the fact that precisely here, in an art focused on narration to an extent found elsewhere only in the Moche Culture of the northern coast of Peru, nothing is known of their divinities. The only thing we know for certain from their art about this light-hearted people is that they had distinct social classes. In their terra-cotta figures, naked men are distinguished from the partly clothed and

Humpback standing on a two-headed fish. Terra cotta, height 16¹⁄₂″. Colima style, culture of the Northwestern Coast, c. 300–1000. From Colima, Mexico. Museo Nacional de Antropología, Mexico, D. F.

from those wearing costly garments and ornaments. The world of this people, as seen in their minor arts, seems quite uncomplicated, but in actuality it was surely far more complex. Their indifference to religion and the loosely organized social structures of their village communities affected their art very little throughout their long span of existence. Their view of the world remained at the stage of preclassic times. It was an age of trial and error, and experimentation went on in this region of the Northwestern Coast throughout the entire classic period up to the arrival of the warlike Tarascans who, with their rigidly organized warrior state, could challenge even the last lords of Mexico, the Aztecs.

Ballplayer. Terra cotta, with red and black paint on a whitish ground, height 17³/₈″. Jalisco style, culture of the Northwestern Coast, c. 300–1000. From the Barrancas region, Jalisco, Mexico. Collection Stendahl, Los Angeles.

Vessel in the shape of an acrobat. Terra cotta, height 6⁵/₈″. Colima style, culture of the Northwestern Coast, c. 300–1000. From Colima, Mexico. Collection Dr. Kurt Stavenhagen, Mexico, D. F.

Most of the art of the Northwestern Coast is typical folk art: naïve, cheerful, optimistic, and entirely spontaneous. The armatures of wire or wooden strips that sculptors today use to hold the clay in form were something that artists of those times did not know. For that reason, at least in the larger figures, it happened often that the wet black clay, still unbaked, sagged down into thick masses. This explains the huge feet (facing page) and thick calves, thighs, and buttocks, which should not, without reservation, be taken to be the ideal of beauty of the time.

The great English sculptor of our century, Henry Moore, once explained that he would never have found the courage to work with "negative space" in his sculpture had he not come across the early Mexican statues in the British Museum. They became more of an influence on him than the work of his contemporary colleagues.

◀ Seated figure, probably symbolizing the ancient fire-god. Volcanic stone, height 12³/₄". Colima style, culture of the Northwestern Coast, c. 300–1000. From Colima, Mexico. Collection Dr. Kurt Stavenhagen, Mexico, D. F.

Seated woman. Terra cotta, height 7". Jalisco style, culture of the Northwestern Coast, c. 300–1000. From Jalisco, Mexico. Collection Dr. Kurt Stavenhagen, Mexico, D. F.

Seated man. Terra cotta with reddish and blackish painting, height 17³/₈″. Jalisco style, culture of the Northwestern Coast, c. 300–1000. From the Barrancas region, Jalisco, Mexico. Collection Stendahl, Los Angeles.

Carved columns which formerly supported the roof of the Palace of Quetzalcoatl, representing the priest-king Quetzalcoatl as the God of the Morning Star. Volcanic stone, height of the figures about 15′9″. Toltec Culture, c. 900–1168. Tula, Hidalgo, Mexico.

Occasional technical deficiencies—apparent only in larger figures—in no way detract from the merit of these daring sculptors of the Northwestern Coast. They knew nothing of the strait-jacket controls of art by religion or state, so in some respects they were ahead of their times, while in others they could not keep step with what was being done elsewhere in Mexico. Only in our century has the fascination of this perfect-imperfect impressionistic art been appreciated again.

The Postclassic period began with the invasion of seminomadic tribes from the north and northwest of Mexico who united in warrior bands and overran and devastated the decadent theocratic centers of the Upper Valley of Mexico. Under the leadership of Mixcoatl ("Cloud-Serpent"), the Nahuatl-speaking Toltecs settled in the Upper Valley and, in a few generations, created the legendary Toltec civilization. Their capital became Tula, earlier known as Tollan ("City-of-Rushes"). In the old sources, there was no other place so often mentioned and so often claimed as their place of origin by every people and every dynasty that had any pride and any pretensions to civilization. In 1168, when new barbarian hordes swept down from the north, the city of Quetzalcoatl, the "Feathered-Serpent," was also ravaged. The priest-king, *Ce Acatl Tolpizin Quetzalcoatl*, to give him his full name, is the first historical personality we can identify in early America. The accounts say he was the fifth overlord of the Toltecs. Around 998 he was driven out of the "City-of-Rushes" by his adversary Tezcatlipoca ("Smoking-Mirror"). Tula is the oldest site in Mexico whose written or oral history has been corroborated, or at least in part supplemented, by archaeological finds.

Tall beaker decorated in relief with, lower middle, two priests and, upper right, Quetzalcoatl performing a ritual act. Earthenware, height c. 10″. Toltec Culture, c. 900–1168. Provenance unknown. Museum für Völkerkunde, Vienna.

Ground plan of Tula (below) and view of the ruins of the Temple of Quetzalcoatl with, in the foreground, the reclining figure of the god Chac-Mool (facing page). Toltec Culture, c. 900–1168. Tula, Hidalgo, Mexico.

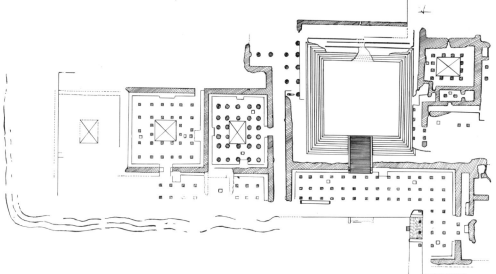

The accounts we have of the Toltecs and their religious center, Tollan, are so shot through with myth that many scholars regarded the Toltec metropolis as little more than a legend. It was an archaeological sensation when methodical diggings were begun in 1940 in Tula and it became certain that the fabulous Tollan of the Toltecs had finally been discovered. There was even a relief which identified Quetzalcoatl as a historical ruler of the city. According to our calendar, his reign began in 980.

Rivalries between military leaders were not rare in Indian history. The struggle that took place in Tula between Tezcatlipoca, the "Smoking-Mirror," and Quetzalcoatl, the "Feathered-Serpent," later made its way into the religious history of the Aztecs. Tezcatlipoca triumphed over Quetzalcoatl and drove him out, together with his followers. Seven hundred and forty-five miles distant from their old home, a new sacred city arose: Chichén Itzá, one of the cities later abandoned by the Mayas (see pages 142–48). Traces of other Toltec tribes who broke away from the Upper Valley have been found on the Pacific side, from Guatemala to Nicaragua. The wide diffusion of Toltec culture is evidenced by formal and stylistic traits in pottery (facing page), in decorative bas-reliefs on buildings, and not least by figures of the gods Quetzalcoatl and Chac-Mool (below).

The last ruler of Tula before its downfall was Huemac. Recent excavations suggest that the Mexicas, or Aztecs, as they called themselves after their mythical original home of Aztlán, may well have played a part in the destruction of the Toltec metropolis.

Toltec art, which is our basic source of information about this scriptless civilization, was in spirit quite opposed to the classic period. From the time of the Toltecs on, religion was at the service of a warrior caste, its task being to glorify war and death: "Then began the time of human sacrifice," as an old record puts it. The reliefs on the walls in Tula express very clearly this new spirit of the times. Reclining figures with more than life-size death's-heads, their bodies partly in the form of serpents, with crossbones as accessory motifs, cover the lengths of the walls (above). Other motifs in frequent use were eagles and jaguars devouring hearts, and these were emblems of the warrior groups. In depictions of animals as well as of death, Toltec art was always rhythmic; in human motifs, however, it remained static. In the past as today—or so it seems—warriors thought to gain some measure of pardon if they showed a human face.

The Aztecs spoke with awe of the Toltecs as a race of artists and builders. Though they had taken part in exterminating the Toltec civilization, the Aztecs admired their defeated enemy. It was as a small minority, the

Standing figure of the god Xólotl. Nephritoid stone with inlays of fragments of shell, height 11¹/₄". Aztec Culture, c. 1370–1521. Provenance unknown. On loan to the Linden Museum, Stuttgart, from the Württemberg Landesmuseum.

Coatepantli, the "Serpent-Wall." Rough stone and baked clay bricks, height of the relief c. 25⁵/₈". Toltec Culture, c. 900–1168. Tula, Hidalgo, Mexico.

last outsiders to arrive before the Spanish conquerors, that the Aztecs came to the fertile Upper Valley of Mexico. They were merely tolerated by their more powerful neighbors, but in a very short time they learned how to assimilate the experiences and achievements of other peoples, and how to improve on them. Heirs of the warlike spirit of the Toltecs, they were both worthy and willing pupils. Wars became more frequent, and sacrifices took on frightful proportions—though not so much as many Spanish chroniclers claimed in an attempt to justify their own cruelty. Artistic activity among the Aztecs, in stone carving at least, reached heights only comparable to those achieved by the Olmecs almost 2,000 years earlier. Sculpture was virtually limited to depictions of gods created for religious purposes, like the Xólotl above. The god is represented almost entirely as a skeleton. He stands for the planet Venus and was considered the companion of the sun on its perilous journey through the death-god's realm of night.

Upper left: Large ceremonial vase with highly stylized serpents' heads. Clay, height 15³/₄″. Aztec Culture, 1370–1521. From the Upper Valley of Mexico. Museo Nacional de Antropología, Mexico, D. F.

Upper right: Mask of a man. Greenish stone, height 5³/₄″. Aztec Culture, 1370–1521. Provenance unknown. Collection Dr. Kurt Stavenhagen, Mexico, D. F.

Head of the moon-goddess Coyolxauhqui. Porphyritic basalt, 30³/₄ × 15³/₈″. Aztec Culture, 1370–1521. From Tenochtitlán. Museo Nacional de Antropología, Mexico, D. F.

Large ceremonial incense burner. Terra cotta, height 45⅝". Aztec Culture, 1370–1521. From Azcapotzalco, Mexico, D. F. Museo Nacional de Antropología, Mexico, D. F.

With the concentration of the population into great cities, artistic ceramics became objects of manufacture. Hundreds, even thousands of small votive figures, which had once been made lovingly by hand, now were mass-produced. Nevertheless, objects of outstanding quality were still turned out for religious use during that period, but they are correctly attributed to Mixtec (facing page, above) or other influences. Only in stone carving were the Aztecs their own masters.

The religion of the Aztecs, like their art in the fifteenth and sixteenth centuries, was a hodgepodge of many, often antithetical, ideas and forms taken over from neighboring peoples and earlier civilizations. There was no true Aztec art, nor can one speak of a purely Aztec religion. Their polytheistic pantheon was crammed with gods from all regions and diverse periods: gods for the heavenly bodies, for the points of the compass, for water, fire, and plant growth, for maize and maguey, for everything in life. With one exception: there was none for love.

Detail view of the fifty-nine-foot-high pyramid of Tenayuca, which was added to eight times. Begun by the Chimimecs between 1064 and 1116, only the final rebuilding was done by the Aztecs. Tenayuca, Upper Valley of Mexico, Mexico, D. F.

Head of a dead man. Basalt, height 12¹/₄″. Aztec Culture, 1370–1521. From the State of Vera Cruz. Museo Nacional de Antropología, Mexico, D. F.

One can search in vain for a Venus in the thirteen heavens and nine underworlds of the Mexicans. Their gods are personifications of the powers of nature. When their sculptors strove to embody in stone these creations of the imagination, the result was that we find, side by side, the poetic and the brutal, purity and horror. The esoteric, complex formal language of the Mayas was alien to the Aztecs. Their statues stress the awesome power of a race that had recently been barbarians, a small and despised tribe which, nevertheless, knew how to impose itself, in less than a century, as the leading nation of Mexico.

Besides monumental architectonic sculpture, there were innumerable depictions of men and gods which are notable for their sensitivity and great simplicity. But there is no laughter in the faces, they scorn pain, and are shut off from feeling. Only rarely is the body shown in action. Once again art reflects its environment; in this case the passive fatalism of the Indians is embodied in their gods. All naturalistic resemblance is severely stylized in this sculpture, made to fit the material in which it is carved; but important details such as garments or ornaments are not neglected.

The water-goddess Chalchiutlicue ("Of-Precious-Stones-Are-Her-Garments"). Basalt, height 15³/₄". Aztec Culture, 1370–1521. Probably from the Upper Valley of Mexico. Museo Regional, Toluca, Mexico.

The bearded god of creation Tonacatecutli ("Lord-of-Our-Flesh"). Basalt, height 13³/₈". Aztec Culture, 1370–1521. Probably from the Upper Valley of Mexico. Museum für Völkerkunde, Basel. Collection Lukas Vischer, 1844.

The dance-god Ixtlilton ("Little-Black-Face"). Basalt, height $17^3/_4''$. Aztec Culture, 1370–1521. Probably from the Upper Valley of Mexico. Museum für Völkerkunde, Basel. Collection Lukas Vischer, 1844.

Man as a mere servant of the gods, as the Aztecs saw it, had little to expect from life. The newborn child was greeted with these highly significant words: "You will know pain and learn to bear it, will see misfortune and abominations. You have come to the place of incessant mourning and affliction where grief is praised, where it is pitiable." True, personal success as warrior or merchant was desirable, but it was of secondary significance only: what counted was service to the gods. "For the sun to illuminate the earth, it must feed on human hearts and drink blood. For this must wars be made, for through them alone can blood and hearts be won. Because all of the gods wished it so, they created war."

One of the rare exceptions in the bloody Olympus of the Aztecs was Ixtlilton, "Little-Black-Face." In the sixteenth chapter of his first book, Father Sahagún says: "He was a god whose temple was built all in wood. . . . Many clay vessels were placed before him. They were called 'his black water.' Whenever a child fell ill, it was brought to Ixtlilton's temple, and the lid of one of the vessels containing black water was opened to let the child drink. And it was cured. . . ."

Head of a monkey. Obsidian, height $3^7/_8$″. Aztec Culture, 1370–1521. Probably from the Upper Valley of Mexico. Museum für Völkerkunde, Vienna.

In the Aztec conception, earthly events were no more than a reflection of the cosmos. With each new day, they observed in the heavens the prototype of their own deeds: the standing war between stars, moon, and sun. Their fanatical religion, combined with their political and military talents, made these young, energetic barbarians one of the most successful peoples of Mexico: new wine in old bottles, as it were. At the time they moved into the fertile Upper Valley of Mexico, all the good places for settlement were already occupied. Nothing was left for the Aztecs except a small swampy island. On it, in 1325, they founded Tenochtitlán, the present-day Mexico City (recent research prefers the date of 1370). What at first seemed a very unpromising site in the middle of Lake Texcoco (which is now arid) turned out to be not only eminently strategic but also highly advantageous. At any time the Aztecs could sweep down from their citadel to war against and plunder other settlements on the shores, or other tribes in the hinterlands. Tenochtitlán itself was virtually impregnable. Only the Spaniards were able to seize it: Cortés had an entire fleet built in the country of the Tlaxcaltecs, transported it secretly across the mountains, and from the lake itself attacked the city a chronicler acclaimed as the "Venice of the New World."

THE MAYAS – STYLES AND CULTURES

Time	Periods	Central Lowland	Highlands of Guatemala and Chiapas	Yucatan
1521		Beginning of the Spanish Conquest		
1400	Postclassic		Xinabahul	Overthrow of Mayapán 1441
1200			Pamplona	Mayapán Fall of Chichén
900		Tepeu	Amatle	Itzá 1194 "League of Mayapán" (987–1185)
600	Classic Age	Tzakol	Esperanza phase	Tulum Chichén Viejo Maya
300			Miraflores	
A.D.				
B.C.				
200	Experimental Age	Chicanel	Kaminaljuyú (Providencia) Sacatepéquez	Dzibilchaltún
600				
900		Mamon-Uaxactún/Tikal	Las Charcas	Early Yucatan
1500			Chiapa de Corzo I	
5000	Early planters			
10000	Hunters and gatherers			

Fragment of a male figure. Terra cotta, height 3¹/₄″. Preclassic Maya Culture, c. 1200 B.C.–A.D. 200. From Honduras. Formerly Staatliches Museum für Völkerkunde, Berlin.

Almost two million Maya Indians still occupy the region in which, throughout fifteen centuries, the most brilliant of all Stone Age cultures flourished. The area shared by some twenty Maya tribes falls geographically into three distinct zones. The earliest region populated was probably the highlands of Guatemala and western El Salvador on the old route to South America. Mexican civilization had no difficulty in influencing this region, but the greatest and most impressive centers of culture grew up in the other two zones.

Seated woman. Terra cotta, height 3¹/₄″. Preclassic Maya Culture, c. 1200 B.C.–A.D. 200. From Juayua, El Salvador. Middle American Research Institute, Tulane University, New Orleans.

The center of Maya culture, spiritually as well as geographically, was the rain forest area, now almost uninhabited, of northern Guatemala, western Honduras, British Honduras, and part of the Mexican states of Chiapas and Tabasco. The boundary of the third zone runs toward the north, roughly where the giant trees of the primeval forest give way to a dense brushwood forest which covers the entire limestone tableland of the Yucatan Peninsula. The oldest evidences of civilization come mostly from the first region. These are statuettes which are smaller relatives of the "pretty ladies" in Mexico (see pages 14–16), and which likewise served mostly as grave offerings.

The young maize-god. Basalt, height 36¹/₄″. Classic Maya Culture, c. seventh–eighth centuries. From Copán, Honduras. British Museum, London.

Stele C with the date of consecration 9. 17. 0. 0. 0. 4 Ahau 18 Muan (A.D. 782). Volcanic stone with traces of reddish paint, height c. 8′ 10″. Classic Maya Culture, Copán, Honduras.

The ball court in Copán, Honduras, with the "Place of the Steles" in the background. Classic Maya Culture, c. fifth–ninth centuries.

One cannot speak of the Maya civilization without mentioning the calendar, an essential feature of their religion. No other people has ever tied up so many mythical and magical conceptions with its notion of time. Dates are incised on almost every building, stairway, and sacrificial altar. The city-states of the classic period erected more than a thousand steles: in the beginning every twenty years, later every ten and sometimes even every five years. On these commemorative pillars are carved long bands of hieroglyphics with calendar reckonings. One of these "time-measures" in Quiriguá, the nearest town to Copán, computes a mythological date going back ninety million years. Only by means of the abstract cipher zero, discovered by the Mayas long before the Asiatic Indians came upon it, could such mathematical problems be solved and, with the help of the movable cipher, be written down. The inscriptions on the steles seen here do not say if the persons represented are meant to be priest-kings or gods.

Full-figured glyph from a sculptured series of glyphs. Limestone, height 9¹/₂″. Classic Maya Culture, A.D. 672. From the palace at Palenque. Museum of Palenque, Chiapas, Mexico.

Temple of the Inscriptions ▶ in Palenque, Chiapas, Mexico. Classic Maya Culture, probably built in the second half of the seventh century.

Glyph representing the sign for the day "9 Ahau." Stucco, height 4³/₄″. Classic Maya Culture, c. seventh–eighth centuries. From Temple XVIII in Palenque. Museum of Palenque, Chiapas, Mexico.

▼

Maya staircases and wall pictures all have a message, but we do not understand it, at least not yet. The most eloquent culture of early America is still silent for us. Only forty per cent of the written signs have been deciphered, mostly numbers and calendar hieroglyphs. The gods here seen in profile wear on their heads the "bundle of time," good and bad times, promising and unpromising. They bear witness to the quest for a divine order, for the understanding of the divine order which reigns over the cosmos and which was such a determining factor in Maya thinking.

The conqueror of Mexico, Hernando Cortés, passed only a few miles from the abandoned religious center of Palenque without even suspecting its existence. Mighty and at the same time beautiful, this gem among Maya cities was built in the midst of nature, in a landscape of which it itself became a part. At the very spot where the flatlands slope gently upward to the mountain of Chiapas, its temples and palaces stretch out in harmonious order. The site was calculated to afford a view over the fields where the peasants tilled the soil. The mountains act as a frame around the places of worship which, like the Greek temples also, were once painted in gleaming colors. While the builders themselves could never have seen their work from a bird's-eye perspective, one has the impression that Palenque was laid out in this way to offer the celestial gods such a view, those very gods who would one day fail it. Like the other city-states, Palenque was abandoned around the ninth century. The primeval forest, which had been cleared with so much toil, then crept back to claim its own. The collapse of the theocratic societies in Mexico, as in Central America, turned the population into nomads. There are many hypotheses as to the real reasons for that collapse: wars, plagues, orders from the gods, exhaustion of the land, any or all of these accompanied by famine and revolution. It is probable, in any case, that the last two causes led ultimately to the downfall of the priestly power and the exodus from the holy places.

Every building in Palenque is a minor work of art. It is the only religious site in which the baroque architecture of the classic period became virtually rococo in style. Not in the height of the base of its pyramid nor in the proportions of its temple can Palenque compete with other cities, but only in the sheer art with which it was built.

Only the actual center, Palenque itself, has been unearthed. Some three to four miles deeper in the forest many smaller constructions still lie hidden. But to lay bare all of it would cost as much as to build a new university, and modern Mexico, which has already spent so much on archaeological research, must give priority to the needs of today.

The palace at Palenque. Classic Maya Culture, c. 400–850. Palenque, Chiapas, Mexico.

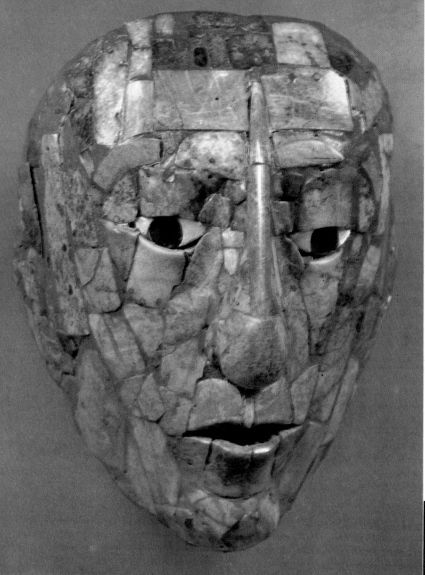

Mask of a dignitary. Jade inlaid with shell, height 11⁷/₈". Classic Maya Culture, c. 692. Found in the crypt of the Temple of the Inscriptions in Palenque, Chiapas. Museo Nacional de Antropología, Mexico, D. F.

Fragment of a male head. Stucco, height 11". Classic Maya Culture, c. 650–750. From Palenque. Museum of Palenque, Chiapas, Mexico.

▼

The Egyptian pyramids were built as tombs for kings, those of America as "mountains for the gods." For centuries now, treasure hunters and scholars alike have combed the Maya temples without ever finding the grave of a king or high priest. So far, the Temple of the Inscriptions is the only exception (see page 103). There, on June 15, 1952, at sixty feet below floor level and six and one-half feet below the base of the pyramid, archaeologists after great labor came upon the undisturbed grave of a high dignitary.

One of the "Nine Lords of the Night." Stucco relief wall decoration, height of the detail c. 19⅝". Classic Maya Culture, c. 692. Crypt of the Temple of the Inscriptions, Palenque, Chiapas, Mexico.

Male head. Stucco, height 11". Classic Maya Culture, c. 692. Found in the crypt of the Temple of the Inscriptions, Palenque, Chiapas. Museo Nacional de Antropología, Mexico, D. F. ▼

The walls of the spacious tomb chamber are decorated with stucco reliefs of the "Nine Lords of the Night" (above). Among the burial offerings were two heads of young men, likewise in stucco (left). The head of the dead official himself was covered by a sumptuous mask in jade (facing page). The nobleman buried in the Temple of the Inscriptions was interred with a splendor unmatched by anything else known in the Maya Culture, and his journey to the other world was accompanied by six young vassals put to death for the occasion.

The Temple of the Cross in Palenque, Chiapas, Mexico. Classic Maya Culture, built in the seventh or eighth century.

Tablet of the Slaves (detail). Limestone, $64^{5}/_{8} \times 59^{1}/_{2}''$. Classic Maya Culture, seventh or eighth century. From Temple XII, Palenque. Museum of Palenque, Chiapas, Mexico.

In Palenque, to write down calendar reckonings, as well as to guarantee the fame of the priest-princes through the ages, there were painted stucco reliefs and limestone tablets (facing page). And yet, one of the twentieth-century descendants of the Mayas was impelled to ask: "But what has become of your sacred princes whose brows were crowned with feathers from all the birds of the world? . . . Itzá is no more and Palenque is no more, where things were done that will never be done again. . . . And Mayapán is no more, the banner and tower of the Mayas. All has passed! Nothing remains but the grave of him who dug the grave. . . ."

Male head. Stucco, height 11″. Classic Maya Culture, c. 700–800. From the Temple of the Sun, Palenque, Chiapas. Museo Nacional de Antropología, Mexico, D.F.

Like Copán and Quiriguá in the eastern Maya territory, in the west there was a similar combination of two stylistically similar religious centers, Palenque and Comalcalco. Their artists preferred limestone or stucco, and these materials were shaped into the most speaking likenesses in all of Maya culture (above). The humanity of these sculptures is quite unexpected in the Americas. No doubt these are portraits of chieftains or priest-princes of the ruling elite. In Palenque and Comalcalco, in contrast to the other cities of the classic period,

Large head of a dignitary. Stucco, height 16⁷/₈″. Classic Maya Culture, c. seventh–eighth centuries. From Comalcalco, Tabasco, Mexico. Museo Nacional de Antropología, Mexico, D.F.

no steles were built. There, reckoning of time was set down on beautiful, sensitively worked bas-reliefs or on semicircular plaques of stucco. The pictographs of Palenque are among the most subtly executed written characters of the entire region. Most of the dates they record fall around the end of the seventh century, though potsherds found in Palenque show that it was a settlement as far back as the preclassic period. Palenque, like the other sacred cities of the lowlands, was abandoned in mid-ninth century.

Receptacle for offerings of feathers, depicting the sun-god. Terra cotta, height 45⅝″. Classic Maya Culture, seventh–eighth centuries. From Palenque, Chiapas. Museo Nacional de Antropología, Mexico, D. F.

Of the religion of the classic period, nothing has come down to us except the images of gods on steles, reliefs, frescoes, and ceramics, and they are difficult to interpret. The only help in identifying a few of the gods comes from oral tradition and accounts written in the postclassic and early colonial periods. Almost all of the divinities incorporate primarily the imaginary forces of nature. They are at one and the same time benevolent and destructive, sometimes one sex, sometimes the other, and not rarely both. They are linked to both heaven and the underworld and play their roles both as living creatures and dead. Along with the rain-god Chac, the sun-god Kinich Ahau was one of the most important deities and legend says it was he who invented poetry. His attribute is the jaguar, and his huge blind eyes make him easily identifiable among the other gods.

Lintel over door no. 26. Stone, dimensions of relief $22^7/_8 \times 27^1/_2''$. Classic Maya Culture, A.D. 720. Yaxchilán, Chiapas, Mexico.

Inaccessible and forbidding in the deep fastness of the jungle is another city in the western part of Maya territory—Yaxchilán. The Usumacinta River makes a horseshoe bend around the spreading range of hills on which this ancient city was laid out. The rain forest has grown over the city so thickly that it cannot be seen either from the river or the air. The artists of Palenque left behind masterworks in stucco, those of Copán ventured so far as to attempt sculpture in the round, but Yaxchilán was unsurpassed in its relief carving. In no other city was such mastery of the flat surface attained, nowhere were bas-reliefs enlivened with such elegance and rhythm. Yaxchilán, also, was not destroyed by war: no traces of violence can be seen. No one can say when or why this very flourishing city was also abandoned in the ninth century.

Fragment of a broken stele. Total height of stele, c. 19′ 8″; height of fragment, 4′ 7¹/₂″. Classic Maya Culture, c. A.D. 700. Bonampak, Chiapas, Mexico.

The discovery of Bonampak in 1945 was a sensation in the world press. A photo-reporter visiting the only still-pagan Indian tribe in Middle America, the Lacandons, learned about the ancient seat of the gods, to which offerings were still brought on certain days. The true name of the city is unknown. Bonampak is a modern name meaning "Painted Walls" in Mayan—an apt name, since its frescoes were what focused world attention on it. They are the most important mural paintings of the Pre-Columbian era in either of the Americas. Technically, they lack perspective and shading, but their drawing is secure and impressive. As in Egyptian and Etruscan murals, the bodies are shown in frontal position, heads and feet in profile. Even the smallest figures thereby acquire, unintentionally it seems, a monumental character. The various functions and ranks of the dignitaries depicted are indicated by their costumes and ornaments. A very few hieroglyphs appear here and there among the figures. One room shows the preparations for a ritual dance, another scenes of fighting, a third the presentation of the captives, and finally their sacrifice.

Wall painting showing three dignitaries. Vegetable and mineral colors applied in fresco technique, height of figures c. 31 ″. Classic Maya Culture, c. A.D. 700. Bonampak, Chiapas, Mexico.

Although no example of a brush has survived, the delicacy of the line drawing shows that these precious frescoes were painted with a fine brush of hair or, at least, with the tail of some animal. The painting was done on a ground of lime one to two inches thick. It was carried out by a group of artists, probably overseen by a master who laid out the composition, drew in the contours, and made the final corrections. As a result of the clearing away of the forest from around the temple and the removal of the protective film of lime built up on the paintings in the course of centuries, the frescoes have suffered greatly in the twenty-odd years since their discovery. It is to be hoped that these unique vestiges of the seventh century may soon be skillfully restored and conserved.

Temple I, also called the Temple of the Great Jaguar, during restoration. Height 154'. Classic Maya Culture, c. 292–850. Tikal, Petén, Guatemala.

Fragment of Stele 29, Volcanic stone, height c. 35″. Classic Maya Culture, A.D. 292. Tikal, Petén, Guatemala.

What Teotihuacán was for Mexico in the classic period, Tikal was for the Maya civilization—a metropolis, a city unsurpassed by any other. In its ruins, which lie at a height of 1,970 feet and are covered over by the rain forest, the earliest date inscribed on any Maya stele was found a few years ago: 8. 12. 14. 8. 15, which in our calendar equals July 6, 292 (left). With this date opens the now virtually complete chronology of the classic period, which lasted until 909. Tikal broke another record: the height of its pyramid, Temple IV, with a height of 258 feet, is by far the tallest construction of Maya times. What distinguishes Tikal from the other cities is its austere and weighty architecture, the impression of power it gives even in ruins. Immensity, force, and cruelty are the concepts, fear and awe the feelings which force themselves on the beholder. The Temple of the Great Jaguar (facing page) and the Temple of the Masks lie on the east-west axis like insurmountable barriers. To the north and south, the rectangular open square is framed by smaller edifices which ingeniously exploit the chain of hills around them to gain height.

It is no wonder that at the beginning of the seventeenth century Father Avendaño, the first European to visit Tikal, should have mistaken these pyramids for hills. "On the tall mountains we passed stand many old buildings, some of which I recognized as dwellings. Because they are very high up and my strength was at an ebb, I climbed up to them only with the greatest difficulty. They are built in the form of a monastery, with many narrow passageways and countless rooms to live in. All of them are roofed over, their interiors whitewashed, and surrounded by a platform. Limestone is more than abundant here, every hill in these regions is composed of it. The buildings here have a form quite different from those in other provinces (Yucatan) where they are put together of hewn stone without mortar—even the arches. Here, the stone walls are all plastered. . . ."

Stone marker for a ball game. Limestone, diameter c. 22″. Classic Maya Culture, A.D. 590. From Chinkultic, Chiapas, Mexico. Museo Nacional de Antropología, Mexico, D. F.

The Olmecs seem to have been the first to make a rubber ball. The extraordinary importance accorded to ballplaying in the later civilizations, in Mexico as well as in Maya territory, is proved by the countless terrains set aside for the sport within the temple areas of the sacred cities. In the Maya towns alone, there are almost fifty. At the basis of the game itself, which was overseen by the priests, lay cosmic conceptions. The ball in flight represented the sun. The ball courts, always oriented toward the northeast, stood for heaven and the underworld. The game symbolized the struggle between light and darkness, summer and winter, life and death. A relief in the ball court at El Tajín shows the leader of the team, how he receives his consecration, and how, when the game is lost, he is offered up as a sacrifice. The player above wears ceremonial clothing, with feathered headdress and loin and thigh guards. The ball was never touched by the hands and could only be butted around by the thighs.

Tripod plate. Painted baked clay, diameter 13 ³/₄". Classic Maya Culture, Tepeu I Phase, 600–675. From Uaxactún, Petén, Guatemala. Museo Nacional, Guatemala.

Like their monumental art, the applied arts of the Mayas also served religion and ritual. Their style varied in different times and places. In the tripod plate above, the priest in the center is encircled by a hieroglyphic inscription. The plate underwent "ceremonial death" before being buried: a hole was bored through it.

Tripod plate decorated with symbolic animals. Painted baked clay, diameter 15³/₄″. Classic Maya Culture, Tepeu I Phase, 600-675. From Uaxactún, Petén, Guatemala. Museo Nacional, Guatemala.

The tripod plate above comes, like the preceding plate, from Uaxactún. It is decorated with an ape and a serpent, two jaguars, and five priests. According to the "Book of Counsel," the Popol Vuh of Quiché-Maya in Guatemala, the ape was the product of the gods' third Creation of Man, which miscarried; it was not until the fourth try that human beings were finally created. In almost all early American cultures, the jaguar symbolizes power and strength. On this plate, the serpent's body divides the highly stylized mythological scene into two worlds, the upper and the lower.

From Uaxactún in the Guatemala lowlands the art of ceramic painting spread to Honduras and El Salvador. It is not known if the people who inhabited what is now El Salvador were at that time of Maya stock. However, the person depicted on the three-legged dish (below) belongs in physiognomy to one of the several ethnic types of the lowland Mayas.

Tripod dish decorated with a human head. Painted baked clay, height 3⁷/₈″. Influenced by classic Maya Culture, c. 500–1000. From San Salvador, El Salvador. Museo Nacional David J. Guzmán, San Salvador.

Plate decorated with figure of a priest. Painted baked clay, diameter 10⁵/₈″. Influenced by classic Maya Culture, c. 500–1000. From San Salvador. Museo Nacional David J. Guzmán, San Salvador.

El Salvador had no architecture on a grand scale comparable to that of the other Maya city-states. But its applied arts, especially its highly stylized pottery painting, scarcely lagged behind that of the other regions. The dancing priest on the tripod plate seen here wears a spendid ceremonial costume of exotic feathers. The inhabitants of the Mexican and Central American highlands especially prized the brilliantly colored feathers of the quetzal bird, whose habitat is the lowlands of Guatemala and Chiapas. Some lists of tribute paid to the Aztecs have survived which show that the defeated tribes were made to pay in quetzal feathers. Moctezuma, the Aztec ruler, gave to the conqueror of Mexico, Hernando Cortés, a headdress of green quetzal feathers. Even today Guatemala is called the "Land of the Quetzal," and its coins use the name of that highly valued bird. In earliest times, trade in feathers for the costumes of the priest-princes must have been carried on in the highlands of El Salvador.

Detail of a pot in human form. Orange-colored baked clay, restored, height c. 9⁷/₈″. Early classic Maya Culture, Esperanza Phase, A.D. 200–500. From Kaminaljuyú, Guatemalan highlands. Museo Nacional, Guatemala.

Like the eastern border regions of Honduras and El Salvador, the Chiapas highlands at the western limits of Maya territory took only a modest part in the cultural progress of the classic culture of the lowlands. Edifices such as those in Palenque and Tikal are lacking there, as are steles like those of Yaxchilán or Copán. Hieroglyphic inscriptions are relatively rare and, when found, use only an ancient, primitive kind of writing. In the expressive pottery of the region there is predominantly Mexican influence: as far back as 2,000 years ago there were elements of Olmec style and later those of the central Gulf Coast, as in this fragmentary head of a maiden.

Head. Baked clay, height c. 11″. Late classic Maya Culture, c. 600–1000. From the Chiapas highlands. Museo Regional de Chiapas, Tuxtla Gutiérrez, Mexico. ▶

Incense burner. Baked clay, height 5″. Early classic Maya Culture, c. 200–500. From Chiapa de Corzo. Museo Regional de Chiapas, Tuxtla Gutiérrez, Mexico.

The Chiapas highlands lie near the Pacific coast and were an old route of passage for a southward migration which preferred this more temperate zone to the almost impenetrable tropical forests. The blackish burned vessel in the form of a man's head (left) was probably used to burn sacrificial offerings such as copal gum. It has a distinct resemblance to similar vessels in the shape of heads which come from the Monte Albán I Culture in the state of Oaxaca, farther to the west. Both objects on this page depict dead persons and reveal the sensitive hand of the Indian artists who, with a minimum of means, understood how to render the tranquil expression of the dead.

In contrast to the expressive naturalism of the Guatemala and Chiapas highlanders, the inhabitants of the Ulua Valley in Honduras achieved an extreme stylization in their applied arts. Pottery painting in that southeastern lowland is unmistakably characteristic and, like the minor arts of Uaxactún, without doubt influenced that of El Salvador. On the jar opposite are depicted pairs of lovers or dancers. Hieroglyphs are not found on ceramics in this region; the scene is framed by a striking ornamental band. Another specialty of the Ulua region is alabasterlike stone vessels with scroll-form decoration and handles carved in the form of jaguars (below). In the late classic period, such vessels were much sought after in trade.

Vase with figured decoration. Baked clay, height 7¹/₄″. Classic Maya Culture, c. 500–800. From Lake Yojoa, Santa Bárbara, Honduras. Middle American Research Institute, Tulane University, New Orleans.

Bearded man. Green mottled stone, height 3″. Classic Maya Culture, c. 500–800. From the Usumacinta region, Chiapas, Mexico. Collection Dr. Kurt Stavenhagen, Mexico, D. F.

In an almost beardless race like the Indian, the rare depiction of a bearded man comes as a surprise. Discoveries such as the man with chin whiskers seen here often give rise to hypotheses that there was some connection between the Old World and the New in the remote past. But there is no scientifically certain evidence of contact with the Vikings from across the Atlantic in the year 1000, nor of any link by way of the Pacific.

Ritual vessel. Calcite, height 10″. Late classic Maya Culture, c. 800–1000. From Ulua Valley, Honduras. The University Museum, Philadelphia.

The so-called Chama Vessel. Painted baked clay, height 9³/₄″. Late classic Maya Culture, Chama III Phase, 600–900. From Chama, Guatemala. The University Museum, Philadelphia.

Quite unlike Ulua ware, the famous Chama Vessel is a remarkable example of a naturalistic trend within classic Maya vase painting. Almost caricatural is this portrayal of priests performing some sort of ceremony. The hieroglyphs, not all of which have been deciphered, probably give the names of these dignitaries. Chama, on the Atlantic side of the Guatemala highlands, was one of the most important manufacturing centers in the classic period.

Ceremonial scenes were frequent subjects for realistically painted pottery; the one above is probably of a religious rite. A priest, with his body painted black, prays for rain and fertility for the crops. This interpretation seems to be borne out by an observation of the American archaeologist Tozzer. During his stay with the only non-Christian Maya Indians, the Lacandons, he found that they made a black paint out of the bister of copal resin and covered their bodies with it for religious ceremonies. This rite is connected with the black rain clouds and the rain-god himself, Mensabak, whose name in the Lacandon language means "The-Maker-of-the-Black-Powder-and-of-Bister."

Detail of a plate. Painted baked clay, shown actual size. Late classic Maya Culture, c. 700–950. From the Campeche coast, Mexico. Collection Manuel Barbachano, Mexico.

Between 700 and 1000, painted pottery went through a renaissance in the Yucatan Peninsula, and once again religious themes were particularly favored. Such religious painting was based on a great number of traditions and conventions at which we can only guess. Certainly the colors must have been chosen for their symbolic significance. Many objects and actions would be inexplicable without this symbolic use of color. Color tells us if the ornaments a dignitary wears are of gold or jade, and what exotic bird furnished the feathers for ritual vestments. Indeed, the symbolism is so far-reaching that the color in which a priest's face is painted tells us which god he served. On frescoes, as in pottery painting, the human face is always presented in profile, the body almost always in frontal position. Portraits, as we think of them in the European tradition, are unknown in early American painting. Nor did artists ever sign their work. Only the style of representation and the technique of execution give us clues as to where and when a work was done.

Two plates. Painted baked clay, diameter of each 11 3/4″. Late classic Maya Culture, c. 700–900. From the Campeche coast, Mexico. Collection Dr. Kurt Stavenhagen, Mexico, D. F.

Priest-prince on his jaguar throne. Painted solid terra cotta, height 4″. Late classic Maya Culture, 700–900. From Jaina Island, Campeche, Mexico. Collection Dr. Kurt Stavenhagen, Mexico, D. F.

Off the coast of the Yucatan Peninsula, on the arid island of Jaina in the Gulf of Campeche, are two ruined Maya pyramids. In the Maya language of Yucatan, Jaina means "The-House-over-the-Sea." But the tiny island does not owe its fame to these pyramids, but rather to the lovely grave offerings which have been dug up by the hundreds and which afford us a glimpse of a long vanished but splendid past. The Jaina terra cottas can be called the Meissen ware of the New World. The figures, mostly of priests, princes, and warriors, are of a harmonious beauty, classic in form and conception. Their calm expressions and dignified bearing suggest an aristocratic self-possession. The modeling of the bodies is restricted to essentials, although it is strongly dynamic, whereas the garments and ornaments which characterize the subject's social rank are worked out in the finest detail. Probably the impressionistic treatment of the bodies was deliberate: it may be that the artists wished to infuse the figures with a breath of that life which death had taken from them—Jaina was not a home for the living, it was an isle of the dead. Most of the dead there were buried in crouching position, and in their mouths was often placed a bead of jade, the stone the Mayas valued higher than gold. In their hands were placed these tiny statuettes which today are sought after as precious rarities.

As in all Maya art, the style of these small terra cottas reflected the spirit of the dominant priestly class or, later, of the aristocracy. The figures provide the strongest evidence of an art based on expression, and mirror the philosophical outlook and religious attitudes of their age as well as its ideal of human beauty. The anonymous artists were almost never given the possibility of infusing their work with their own ideas. They were no more than the hands which executed the ideas of the class that held the power.

Diego de Landa, who was the Spanish bishop in Yucatan in the sixteenth century, related that the artists withdrew to their houses, where they fasted, practiced strict continence in every respect, and were made to perform rigorous rituals until such time as their work was completed. If they violated these ascetic rules in any way, their work was judged unclean, and this the community took as an evil omen. No source tells us whom the Jaina figures were meant to portray: relatives of the dead man, gods and goddesses, or symbolic effigies of the ruling class. Unlike the practice in other cultural centers, these grave offering were not "killed," that is, broken or pierced, but confided to the dead person intact.

Aristocratic woman and dignitary. Painted solid terra cotta, height 7″. Late classic Maya Culture, 700–900. From Jaina Island, Campeche, Mexico. Collection Dr. Kurt Stavenhagen, Mexico. D.F.

Detail of a warrior. Solid terra cotta, height of detail 5$^1/_2$″. Late classic Maya Culture, 700–900. From Jaina Island, Campeche, Mexico. Collection Dr. Kurt Stavenhagen, Mexico, D.F.

The conspicuous place allotted to warriors in the Jaina terra cottas allows us to conclude that, contrary to the opinion of many historians, there must have been a great many wars between the individual city-states during the Maya classic period. True, we have no written records from that time, but it is likely that the Maya hieroglyphs, most of which have not yet been deciphered, tell of such wars. As we know from the Chilam Balam, the books of the jaguar-priests which were written in the Maya language of Yucatan but with European characters, the centuries before the Spanish colonization were anything but peaceful.

Seated dignitary. Solid terra cotta, height 5⁷/₈″. Late classic Maya Culture, 700–900. From Jaina Island, Campeche, Mexico. Collection Stendahl, Los Angeles.

Anonymity was the fate not only of the artists who made the Jaina terra cottas but also of the priests and rulers of the classic period whom they portray. But these miniature statuettes from the isle of the dead, done between the fifth and tenth centuries, do tell us what the elite of the time considered beautiful in the human person. They are model types, as it were, of the builders and inhabitants of those abandoned cities, and they show what warriors and priests looked like, how the nobles dressed. Dignified and aloof, only very rarely do these statuettes depict the lower classes.

Aristocratic woman. Terra cotta, height 8⁵/₈″. Late classic Maya Culture, 700–900. From Jaina Island, Campeche, Mexico. Museo Nacional de Antropología, Mexico, D.F.

At least a quarter of the grave objects found on Jaina are of remarkable quality. They are beautiful, like this distinguished lady, and beautiful according to the aesthetic standards of Europe. Everything about them is harmonious, classically balanced in conception as in form.

Woman seated on a dais. Solid terra cotta, height 4³/₄". Late classic Maya Culture, 700–900. From Jaina Island, Campeche, Mexico. Collection Dr. Kurt Stavenhagen, Mexico, D. F.

For all that they reflect the haughty dignity of the priestly class, the Jaina terra cottas are in no way enigmatic and appeal even to the layman. There is nothing in them of the oppressive anxiety we associate with the tropics nor the profound mysticism of Maya art from other localities. We feel that beneath the skin of this woman blood once pulsed, and we sense in her face the emotions she must have felt: happiness, melancholy, fixity of purpose, and, not least, pride. Like the temples and palaces, these statuettes were originally painted in luminous colors.

Ceremonial axes (*hachas*) comprise a separate category of Maya applied arts. Their specific form must have originated in the central Gulf Coast. It is surprising that the *hacha* was the only form used wherever Maya culture prevailed; other types predominant on the Gulf Coast were not adopted by the Mayas. The war ax below is in the shape of a bird's head, the one on the opposite page in the form of a warrior's head with a jaguar-head helmet. They are grave offerings from the Guatemala highlands, though probably not importations but made there by Maya sculptors. As on the Gulf Coast, the motifs are generally stylized animal or human heads, probably emblems of various warrior castes.

◀ Ceremonial ax. Green mottled granite, height 11″. Late classic Maya Culture or early postclassic period, c. eighth–twelfth centuries. From San José, Guatemala highlands. Collection Carlos Nottebohm, Guatemala.

Ceremonial ax. Gray granite, height 9⁷/₈″. Late classic Maya Culture or early postclassic period, c. eighth–twelfth centuries. From San José, Guatemala highlands. Collection Carlos Nottebohm, Guatemala.

THE POSTCLASSIC PERIOD

Sometime around the ninth century, in a kind of chain reaction which took place almost simultaneously, the theocratic societies collapsed throughout Mexico and Central America. Afterward, the center of Maya civilization was displaced to the north, to the Yucatan Peninsula. There, after a silence of more than a century, art began to flourish anew. On the waterless limestone tableland of the peninsula, men could survive only in the vicinity of *cenotes,* as the Mayas called the natural hollows where the soil had given way down to underground slurces of water. Around these craters rose the cities of the postclassic period, and they were no less splendid than those of classic times. Where priest-princes had earlier held sway over human life from birth to death, now there were secular rulers who once again demanded atrocious sacrifices from their subjects to built new pyramids and mightier palaces.

Now the chief concern of life became the success or failure of the harvest. The rain-god Chac, who had the power to let the maize grow or to destroy it, was the divinity most often depicted in the art of the arid penin-

"Codz Pop" (The House of the Masks) at Kabáh, Yucatan, Mexico. Early postclassic period, Puuc style, c. 1000–1200.

Arch of Labná, Yucatan, Mexico. Early postclassic Maya Culture, Puuc style, c. eleventh–thirteenth centuries.

sula. Codz Pop, the House of the Masks, is the name the Yucatan natives give to the 147-foot-long building in Kabáh. Its façade, facing west, is decorated with innumerable masks of the rain-god, who in this region was always depicted with a long trunklike snout. In both the architecture and minor arts of many cities of Yucatan, the Toltecs who moved in from Mexico replaced the image of this god, which always assumes geometrical forms, with another fertility symbol, that of the Feathered-Serpent.

The so-called Arch of Labná (below), with its corbeled vault, is one of the most remarkable examples of postclassic architecture. The true vault, as developed in ancient Italy, appeared in America only with the Spaniards. But the promise of a great renaissance in architecture, whose beginnings are particularly evident in the postclassic cities of Yucatan, was not fulfilled. As early as two centuries after its first appearance, there are obvious signs of exhaustion. Like the sacred cities of the classic period before them, Labná, Uxmal, and Kabáh were abandoned around the thirteenth century. We know that the Xui dynasty of the state of Uxmal built a new residence deeper in the interior and—prophetically—gave it the name Mani, which in Maya is tantamount to saying "it is done with."

The House of the Dwarf (west façade), Uxmal, Yucatan, Mexico. Early postclassic Maya Culture, c. 950–1250, Puuc style.

In Uxmal it becomes especially clear that the typical arrangement of many Maya cities is vertical. Indeed, height is the index of the importance of a building. According to an old legend, the highest pyramid in Uxmal was called the House of the Dwarf (but also the Pyramid of the Soothsayer). It can be seen from everywhere in the city, and from every vantage point this strangely haunting construction gives the same impression of being forbidding and inaccessible. The two halls used for religious ceremonies are reached by 118 steps. Masks of the rain-god Chac line the steep stairway on the western side (facing page). Five superstructures and additions can be made out in this pyramid. The first temple is almost at ground level, the second can be reached only by the stairway on the east side, while the third is concealed within the bulk of the pyramid and is invisible from outside. The fourth temple was added to the west side (facing page), and the broad surface of the fifth addition crowns the entire elliptical pyramid.

The "Castillo" seen from the Temple of the Warriors

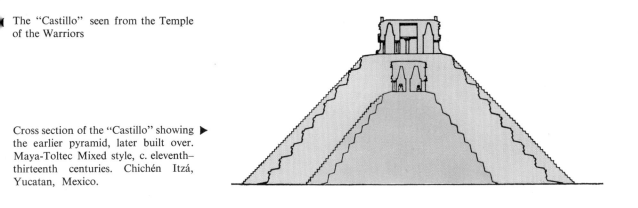

Cross section of the "Castillo" showing ▶ the earlier pyramid, later built over. Maya-Toltec Mixed style, c. eleventh–thirteenth centuries. Chichén Itzá, Yucatan, Mexico.

In the northern lowland of Yucatan lies one of the earliest settlements, Chichén Itzá ("At-the-Well-of-Itzá"). Founded in the sixth century, the city did not attain its great importance until sometime between the eleventh and thirteenth centuries, when the Toltec tribe, driven out of Tula some 745 miles distant, settled there and, by their union with the natives, created a mixed culture. The Castillo (facing page) and the Temple of the Warriors (below), along with other edifices, were then rebuilt in Toltec style. The great columns and heads, always in the form of serpents, represent Quetzalcoatl, the Feathered-Serpent, the half-mythical ruler and culture hero of the Toltecs, whose name in Yucatan was altered to Kukulkán without changing its meaning.

In the foreground the base of the stairway of the Castillo, in the background the Temple of the Warriors, Chichén Itzá, Yucatan, Mexico. Maya-Toltec Mixed Culture, c. eleventh–thirteenth centuries.

The "Caracol," the observatory at Chichén Itzá, Yucatan, Mexico. Maya-Toltec Mixed Culture, c. eleventh–thirteenth centuries.

The astronomical observatory at Chichén Itzá has been named the Snail House—"Caracol"—because of its helicoid form. A passageway in the interior slopes gently upward in a spiral (see diagram at right). Only twice a year does the sun penetrate into the interior through the narrow slits of windows, and then only for seconds at the most. As simple a process as it is reliable, this was how the Maya priests in Chichén Itzá measured the passage of time.

Mexican architectural forms such as the circular plan of the Caracol, architectonic elements like the pillars of the Temple of the Warriors, and the great religious veneration paid to the jaguar—all of these show how much the Toltec spirit differed from the Maya. At the start of the thirteenth century Chichén Itzá was once again abandoned. However, it remained a holy place to which, as late as 1536, pilgrims still came from every corner of Maya territory. In the early part of our century, archaeologists found in the sacred well at Chichén Itzá offerings in the form of ceramic, jade, copper, and gold objects, but also forty-two skeletons of human beings sacrificed to the rain-god. Scholarly research into the finds has not been able to refute the legend that innumerable maidens were sacrificed in the sacred well, though of the forty-two skeletons found there only eight were female.

Jaguar throne of a high dignitary, from inside the "Castillo," Chichén Itzá, Yucatan, Mexico. Red-painted massive stone with green jade inlays. Maya-Toltec Mixed Culture, c. eleventh–thirteenth centuries.

Miniature decorative shield. Wood with pyrite and turquoise inlay, diameter 7′ 11¹/₄″. Postclassic Maya period with Toltec influence, c. twelfth century. From Chichén Itzá, Yucatan, Mexico. Museo Nacional de Antropología, Mexico, D.F.

On this ceremonial shield found at Chichén Itzá, the four "Fire-Serpents" in mosaic probably represent the four points of the compass. In pre-Toltec times, the cardinal directions were symbolized by different colored masks of the rain-god Chac, as we know from the structure called the "Iglesia" (facing page). In pictographs,

"La Iglesia," Chichén Itzá, Yucatan, Mexico. Late classic Maya Culture, c. 600–950.

the rain-gods are identified by their color: red for East, white for North, black for West, yellow for South. Those same colors were used on the façades of Maya buildings which, like those of ancient Greece, were originally brightly painted.

Tomb in Balancanché, Yucatan, Mexico. Toltec Culture, c. eleventh–thirteenth centuries.

Ten years ago archaeologists found a totally undisturbed burial place only two and one-half miles from Chichén Itzá. The entrance was barred by roughly cut blocks of stone. Innumerable clay vessels, many decorated with the face of the Mexican rain-god Tlaloc, as well as millstones for grinding maize (*metates*), were buried with the dead in the red stalactite cave of Balancanché. The style of the vessels indicates that this was a purely Toltec burial place.

The Maya system of writing was more than pictographic. In fact, of the more than 123 different tribal groups inhabiting both Americas before the Conquest, the only ones to work out a true script were the Mayas. "These people use definite signs or letters to record in their books their early history and their lore. By means of those letters, as well as by drawings and figures, they can understand their own story and make others understand and learn from it. We found a great number of books, and since there was nothing in them but superstitions and the lies of the devil, we burned them all, to the great woe and lamentation of the people."

Those sentences were written in 1556 by Bishop Diego de Landa, when he was ordered back to Spain. In them he hoped to justify his harsh measures against the inhabitants of the conquered territory of Yucatan. No one at that time could imagine what irreparable blows to knowledge were caused by the religious zeal of the Spaniards. Only three manuscripts were saved from the holocaust, and they found their way to Europe, ending up in Madrid, Paris, and Dresden. The Dresden Codex (below and next page) surpasses by far in both age and artistic quality the other two manuscripts. This folding book seems to concern the periods of rotation of the planet Venus, but unfortunately only about a third of the Maya hieroglyphs have been deciphered. For that reason, what moves us most in it is its artistic subtlety.

Detail from the Dresden Codex showing a god holding a sacred vessel. Hammered plant fibers covered with a thin chalk ground, dimensions of detail $1^7/_8 \times 2''$. Provenance unknown. Maya Culture, c. tenth–twelfth centuries. Sächsische Landesbibliothek, Dresden.

Two pages of the Dresden Codex. Hammered plant fibers covered with a thin chalk ground, height 8″. Provenance unknown. Maya Culture, c. tenth–twelfth centuries. Sächsische Landesbibliothek, Dresden.

THE LANDS OF GOLD

FROM NICARAGUA TO COLOMBIA

The several "Lands of Gold"—southern Nicaragua, Costa Rica, Panama, and Colombia—were both bridges and barriers between the two chief centers of Indian civilization. The Atlantic side is covered by an almost impenetrable rain forest which sheltered a seminomadic Indian population. On the Pacific side, separated from the tropical rain forest by a mountain chain, there developed a higher civilization. The burial places of these regions have given up their secrets and their treasures almost exclusively to the "huaqueros," the freebooting native treasure hunters. In only a few places were scholars able to forestall the grave looters. As a consequence, it is almost impossible to date anything with precision. What is more, since the trade routes between the higher civilizations to the north (Mexico) and the south (Peru) led through this region, it is difficult to say positively just what originated in the Lands of Gold and what was brought in.

NICARAGUA TO COLOMBIA – STYLES AND CULTURES

Time	Nicaragua	Costa Rica	Panama	Northern Colombia	Central and Southern Colombia
1500	↑	↑	↑	↑	↑
	Managua style	Late Nicoya	Late Coclé	Sinú style	Muisca
1200	Late Nicoya	Chiriquí	Chiriquí/Veraguas	Tairona	Chibcha of Bogotá
					Quimbaya
1000			Middle Coclé	Rio Magdalena style	Colima style
700					
	Early Nicoya	Early Nicoya			
500			Early Coclé		
200					Tierradentro
A.D.					San Agustín
B.C.					
200					

152

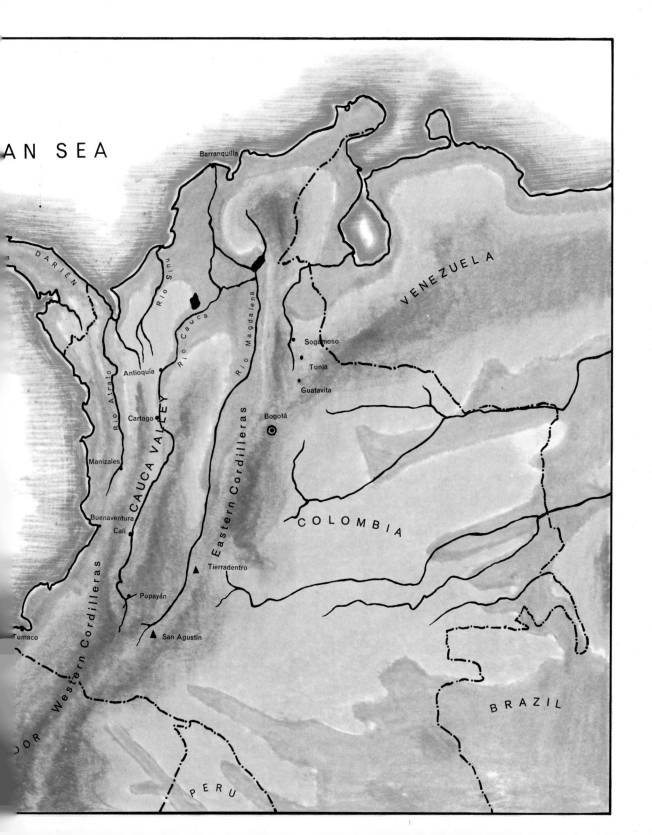

AN SEA

Barranquilla

DARIEN

Rio Sinú

Rio Cauca

Rio Atrato

Rio Magdalena

VENEZUELA

Sogamoso

Tunja

Guatavita

Antioquía

Cartago

CAUCA VALLEY

Bogotá

Eastern Cordilleras

Manizales

Buenaventura

Cali

COLOMBIA

Tierradentro

Popayán

San Agustín

Tumaco

Western Cordilleras

DOR

BRAZIL

PERU

In Colombia and Panama the Chibcha tribes were the leading cultural force, and among them the foremost group was the Muisca. They settled in the high valleys near the present-day capital of Bogotá, and their culture developed in the *tierra fria*, the cold climate of the Eastern Cordilleras, a region between 6,500 and 9,800 feet above sea level. What is perhaps the strangest, most exotic art of Pre-Columbian America comes from the Isthmus region. Just as Costa Rica and the land bridge of Panama link the two subcontinents, so also the craftsmen of those countries combined elements of the northern and southern cultures into a powerful, individual style. The forms and decorative motifs of their works in clay, gold, and stone make up a pantheon of supernatural fantastic creatures: alligators with human bodies, four-headed birds of prey, jaguars crouching for attack with claws and fangs and bulging eyes, and, above all, trophy heads as a sign of the power of their talons. Every art object in these regions is overladen with symbols which reflect the unrestrained exuberance of nature in the tropics.

North of Costa Rica the number of gold objects that have been found decreases, and there are mostly stone statues and brightly painted pottery. Many of the works in clay are painted by a kind of stencil process: parts of the vessel are covered with wax, and when the vessel is dipped into paint the parts covered by wax remain the original color of the baked clay. This technique seems to have spread northward from Peru.

A typical mountain landscape in Colombia.

Mythical animal, probably an ape. Painted terra cotta, height 8⅝". c. 900–1400. From Rivas–Nicoya region, borderland of Nicaragua and Costa Rica. Collection Mario Belli, Managua, Nicaragua.

Standing jaguar. Painted terra cotta, height 12½". c. 900–1400. From Filadelfia, Guanacaste, Costa Rica. Collection Stendahl, Los Angeles.

Tripod dish in jaguar form. Painted terra cotta, height 5⅞". c. 900–1400. From Rivas–Nicoya region, borderland of Nicaragua and Costa Rica. Collection Mario Belli, Managua, Nicaragua.

On the southern shore of Lake Nicaragua and on the Nicoya Peninsula of Costa Rica lived the Chorotega and Nicarao tribes who, in language, were related to the Mexican Otomí and the Nahua. The vividly colored and highly imaginative ceramics seen here are attributed to them. The forms and decorative motifs belong to a world of fantastic creatures. Jaguars (above and left) are tricked out with human attributes, and apes (facing page) are bedecked with countless symbols drawn from the mysteries of tropical nature which have a religious significance we today can scarcely begin to fathom.

Jar in the form of a face. Painted terra cotta, height 8¼″. c. 800–1200. From Línea Vieja, Costa Rica. Museo Nacional de Costa Rica, San José.

In the Isthmus region, as everywhere else in early America, a distinction can be made between ordinary pottery for domestic use and qualitatively better ceramics intended for burial rites. However, all clay vessels of any type whatsoever were made without the help of the potter's wheel, an invention unknown in America before the Spaniards came. The Indian potter kneaded clay into snakelike strips which he then coiled around in spirals to the desired form. Separate parts of the body, such as the nose, mouth, eyebrows, and ears, were then usually modeled directly in the clay, as in the example above. After a brief drying, the vessel was painted. Through carefully controlled firing at a high temperature with uniform oxygenation, the quartz particles in the clay became fused and formed a kind of glaze. To heighten the sheen of the surface, it was also polished by hand with smooth stones.

Kneeling figure. Painted ceramic, height 8¼". c. 200–500. From Nicoya Peninsula, Costa Rica. Museo Nacional de Costa Rica, San José.

Human beings were depicted much less often than mythical animals in this region. When they appear, they probably always represent chieftains (above). The incised lines indicate tattoo marks, and the yellow circles in low relief stand for disk-shaped gold ornaments.

With Costa Rica and the Isthmus of Panama forming a corridor linking the two subcontinents, the Pre-Columbian craftsmen in this area synthesized elements from both the north and the south into a regional style which was both independent and distinctive. That is why the vessel in the shape of a duck (below) shows such astonishing similarities to Peruvian pottery. On the other hand, there are painted designs on the face and body of the seated male figure (above), of the sort used by inhabitants of all parts of the Americas. The oldest example of such designs is found in Tlatilco pottery in Mexico from around 1200 B.C., and they are still used by the forest Indians of the Guaiacas tribe, who live in the border zone between Venezuela and Brazil.

Seated male figure. Reddish painted terra cotta, height 7¼". c. 500–1000. From Nicoya, Costa Rica. Museo Nacional de Costa Rica, San José.

Duck. Painted terra cotta, height 4". c. 500–1000. From Miravalles region, Costa Rica. Museo Nacional de Costa Rica, San José.

In Panama and Colombia the Chibcha tribes were the most culturally advanced. They were remarkable above all for their great skill as goldsmiths. The techniques they employed probably initiated in Peru, but spread across Colombia and Central America into Mexico. Proof of this is that in the Chavín Culture of the northern highlands of Peru artistic work in gold can be found as far back as 500 B.C., though it did not appear in Mexico until 1,400 years later. In the Isthmus regions, the provinces of Veraguas and Coclé in Panama were the great centers for goldsmith work. Through commerce, examples of this work were spread as far abroad as Yucatan. The typical "Gold Eagle" design (below), found frequently, was mentioned by Columbus as a pectoral ornament worn by the chieftain there.

▲
Amulet. Cast gold, height 2³/₄″. c. 1000–1500. From Coclé region, Panama. Brooklyn Museum, New York.

Pendant. Gold cast in a single piece, height 6″. Style of Veraguas, Panama. Textile Museum, Washington, D.C.

Vase. Painted baked clay, height 8″. c. 500–1250. From Coclé, Panama. Brooklyn Museum, New York.

A special trait of Coclé ceramics is their harmonious soft coloring. The fame of that province, which lies northwest of Veraguas, is due as much to its vases and bowls as to its gold ornaments, shell inlays, bone carvings, and work in precious and semiprecious stones. Radiocarbon dating tests place the beginnings of this culture in the third century of our era. However, stylistic resemblances to objects found in graves of an earlier period prove that the Coclé Culture actually goes much further back. An earlier phase known to us had neither metalwork nor painted pottery. No stone buildings or larger architectural constructions are known in the region between El Salvador and Colombia before the Conquest. No people in this area was ever organized into a state, properly speaking. The tribes remained in the primitive stage of a barbarian culture led by chieftains and shaman priests. The only exceptions were a few Chibcha tribes in Colombia, in which one can recognize the rudiments of some sort of notion of a state.

Colombia has considerably more than one and one-half times the area of Texas and resembles an immense mosaic which has remained unfinished. While elsewhere in Latin America archaeological research was carried out energetically after World War II, it stagnated in the fourth largest country of South America. The years of the *violencia*, the bloody guerilla war which between 1948 and 1958 cost over 200,000 lives, are not yet ended. Many valleys of considerable importance to archaeology are still controlled by bandits.

If there is scarcely one country in Latin America which resembles any other in geography, in Colombia there are not even two provinces which are geographically alike. The province of Antioquía was at the time of the Conquest the home of the Quimbayas, the finest goldsmiths of South America. Almost all the techniques practiced today were known to them, including that of the copper-gold alloy which they called *tumbaga*. But they left behind them no ruins of villages or places of worship, no traces of their existence other than their graves.

The Quimbaya style differs from all other Colombian styles in its emphasis on realism. Nothing is transformed into the demoniac or the abstract. The typical figures of the "caciques," their chieftains, are mostly nude except for a gold helmet and chains of gold beads around the neck, calves, and ankles. Female figures are rare. And yet, remarkable as is the Quimbaya goldsmith work, their pottery can only be called primitive.

Figure of a standing nude cacique holding two calabashes from which project spatulas used to scoop out the chalk which was chewed together with coca leaves. Gold cast by the lost-wax method (690 grams). Quimbaya style, c. eleventh–fifteenth centuries. From Antioquía, Central Cauca Valley, Colombia. Formerly Staatliches Museum für Völkerkunde, Berlin.

Mask, probably a death mask. Cold-hammered gold (79 grams), height 7″. c. 900–1400. From Calima region, Upper Cauca Valley, Colombia. Formerly Staatliches Museum für Völkerkunde, Berlin.

It was not without reason that the Spaniards combed Colombia in search of El Dorado, the land of the gilded caciques. The clue was given by a prince of Guatavita. For special solemnities his entire body was covered with a resinous salve and then powdered over with gold dust. In sunlight he seemed to be the god himself. After performing the sacrifice, he was given a ritual bath. This custom became known abroad by hearsay and gave rise to the legend of El Dorado, the Land of Gold. Colombia has remained the land of gold even in our time—its currency is backed up by the national bank with the grave offerings of pre-Hispanic Quimbaya and Muisca princes.

Gold was washed out of streams as well as mined from ore. To reach the veins of gold, steep-sided running trenches were dug, so narrow that only one person at a time could enter. Knowledge of the extraction and preparation of gold probably spread from Peru across Colombia and Central America, at last to reach Mexico. In the Chavín Culture, the art of the goldsmith can be traced back as far as 500 B.C., whereas in Mexico it did not become known for another 1,400 years. Only the copper and gold alloy called *tumbaga* (facing page, below) was a purely Colombian discovery.

At the time of the Spanish Conquest, only two regions in Colombia had achieved a cultural development which raised them above the level of the tropical agricultural societies. In the central and southern Cauca Valley was the home of the Quimbaya Culture and the Calima style (above). No tribal name has been associated with the Calima style, and the once mighty Quimbayas are now extinct. The other region, the highland around Bogotá, was the seat of various Chibcha tribes constituting many separate small states. Probably, had it not been for the incursion of the Spaniards, they would in time have combined into a single unified state like that of the Incas.

Ornamental pendant depicting two mythological beings. Gold cast by the lost-wax method, height 2³/₄". Darién style, c. 1200–1500. From Northwest Colombia. Brooklyn Museum, New York.

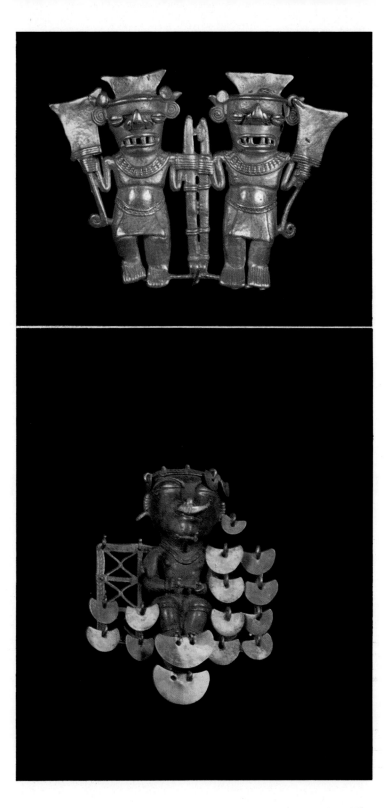

Ornamental pendant. *Tumbaga* (copper-gold alloy) cast by the lost-wax method with separate pieces in hammered gold soldered on, height 4³/₄". Quimbaya style, c. eleventh–fifteenth centuries. From Central Cauca Valley, Colombia. Brooklyn Museum, New York.

Demon. Stone, height about 59″. San Agustín Culture, without precise dating, probably first millennium A.D. San Agustín, Colombia.

Demon. Stone, height 31 1/2".
San Agustín Culture, without precise dating, probably
first millennium A.D. San
Agustín, Colombia.

In an area of about 193 square miles in the highest part of the Magdalena Valley, there are found remains of a very ancient culture. It seems almost as if the representatives of that culture considered only stone statuary as fit to express their religious feelings. Of the more than 300 statues found so far, the great majority are of humans with animal attributes. The depiction of clothing and accessories on these zoomorphic monuments varies, but the characteristic elements—the broad, flat nose and the wide mouth with teeth protruding as in a beast of prey—remain constant. The exaggeratedly prominent fangs are associated with the divine function of the personage depicted (above and facing page). The wide nostrils of these nameless gods have suggested to many scholars that San Agustín must have been the religious center for a Negroid population. There is, however, no proof of this, and animal figures done by the same people have the same broad noses.

If one compares the style and motifs of other American cultures with those of these large statues and the local architecture—which latter was purely megalithic since masonry was not employed—it becomes clear that the San Agustín Culture was oriented toward the south. The closest parallel in style and conception to this Colombian art is found in Chavín de Huántar in the northern highlands of Peru. But in the earliest phases of many other American cultures there was the same profound religious veneration of the puma. Only as the gods became differentiated in the theocratic societies did this cult decline. Thus, in Central America the "Tiger-Face" of the Olmecs later became the rain-god Chac of the Mayas.

A cacique. Terra cotta with red ocher painting, height 9¹/₂". Muisca style, c. 1200–1500. Probably from the highlands near Bogotá. Linden Museum, Stuttgart.

Religious themes from the time before the Conquest are rare in Colombian pottery. There were either the simplest sort of pots or grave offerings with figures of rulers and warriors or, occasionally, animals. Despite the great technical skill of the Muiscas, their pottery was characteristically monochromatic. The figures lack individualistic features, and all naturalistic resemblance was avoided. This would not necessarily be a negative trait if within such a style variation and experimentation were attempted. But to have seen one of these pieces is to have seen them all (above). However, for their part, the ceramics of Tumaco are entirely different. They try to pin down every individual feature of the person depicted. Tumaco lies in the southwest corner of Colombia, close to the border of Ecuador. That is why the closest parallels to Tumaco ware are not to be found in Colombia but farther south, in the Esmeraldas style of Ecuador.

THE EMPIRE OF THE INCAS

FROM ECUADOR TO CHILE

To understand the diversity of cultures in the Central Andes area, one must keep in mind the geography. The coastal region stretches over twenty degrees latitude and is wasteland except for the river valleys. It could scarcely provide the means of subsistence for a sizable population had not the inhabitants in earliest times made the river oases fruitful by digging immense irrigation ditches, one of them more than 435 miles in length, some of which are still in use today. Directly behind the coast the Andes rise up steeply, their highest peaks soaring to over 19,700 feet. Between the separate mountain chains lie high valleys and plateaus. To the east, the Andes drop abruptly to the primeval tropical forest of the Amazon headwaters. The great disparity in height between mountains and coastal regions was, as it happened, far less of an obstacle to the spread of a culture than were the trackless wastes between the valleys on the coast. It was not until the Incas rose to power in the last centuries before the Spanish Conquest that the entire area became a cultural, political, and military unity. A major factor in this cohesion was the Incas' wide-flung network of roads stretching across the wastelands, a network which in both length and excellence far surpassed anything the Romans built.

But before the Incas, various distinct styles had developed contemporaneously within the narrow confines of the geographically isolated valleys and plateaus. Therein lies one of the chief explanations for the immense diversity of early Peruvian art which, in spite of many suggestive ideological and technological similarities, is basically different from what developed in other parts of the Americas.

ANCIENT PERU – STYLES AND CULTURES

Time	Periods	Northern Coast	Northern Highland	Central Coast	Central Highland	Southern Coast	Southern Highland
1532–34		Spanish Conquest					
1440	Imperialist city builders	Inca	Inca	Inca	Inca	Inca	Inca
1200	Period of expansion	Chimu	Huamachuco	Chancay	Early Inca	Ica	Chullpa
1000		Huari	Wilkawain	"Epigonal"	Huari	"Epigonal"	"Epigonal"
800		"Epigonal"——Tiahuanaco——Tiahuanaco———————————Tiahuanaco——Tiahuanaco					
500	"Golden Age"						Classical Tiahuanaco and Huaraz
200		Moche				Nazca	
				Early Lima		Paracas Necropolis	Pacava
A.D.	Experimental Period						
B.C.		Vicús				Paracas Cavernas	Chiripa
300		Gallinazo					
800	Religious	Salinar	Chavín de Huántar	Early Ancón		Cerrillos (Chavín influence)	
		Cupisnique					
1500	Formative	Guañape		Asia			
3500	Early planters	Huaca Prieta					
9000	Hunters and gatherers	San Pedro de Chicama	Lauricocha				Ayampitín

Inca citadel of Machu Picchu
in the Peruvian highlands

To guarantee a wide diffusion of the ideas of a people, the invention of an impressive and understandable image of divinity was, in an art based on religion, just as important as the development of technical craftsmanship. Both elements were present in the Chavín Culture, named after the sacred city of Chavín de Huántar in the northern highlands. With the aid of a highly individual style, unique both artistically and technically, the Chavín religious conceptions, which were centered in veneration of a puma-god, spread over the entire northern and central coasts sometime around the middle of the first millennium B.C. Traces of the influence of the religious notions held by this first higher civilization can be found even in the southern region.

As in Mexico, in what is called the Olmec Culture (see pages 19–27), here too the perfection achieved right from the outset is astounding. A number of innovations aided in this expansion, which was led by the small dominant class of priests and whose impact must have been felt in the religious sphere more than the military. As far as we know today, the earliest Peruvian civilization was that of Chavín which, in the coastal area, is known as Cupisnique after the chief site explored there. The jaguar, in highly stylized form, is found on its woven cloths, clay vessels (facing page), metalwork (facing page), and stone reliefs. Only in later times was this zoomorphic god depicted with somewhat more realism, though never in truly naturalistic guise.

Typical of the Chavín style in pottery are vessels in heavy clay with a hooped handle serving also as a spout. Such spouts in the form of a stirrup ring remained a specialty of the northern coast through all the cultures right up to the Conquest (left). The contours, decorative reliefs, and incised designs of these vigorous, forceful ceramics generally assume spiral forms. Any hint of realism is carefully avoided, and without doubt the abstract "signs" typical of their decoration must also have had some magical significance.

Vessel with stirrup-ring spout and lightly modeled relief decoration. Baked clay, partly polished, height 11 3/4″. "Epigonal" Chavin Culture of the coast, Cupisnique style, c. 600–200 B.C. From northern coast of Peru. Museo Arqueológico de la Universidad Nacional de Trujillo, Peru.

Head of a puma. Hammered silver, height 8″. Chavín Culture, Cupisnique style, c. 600–200 B.C. From Pachacamac, central coast of Peru. Museum of Natural History. New York.

Globular jug with hoop between handle and spout. Baked clay, height 6¹/₄″. Paracas Cavernas Culture, Ocucaje style, c. 500–100 B.C. From Chiquerillo, Ica Valley, southern coast of Peru. Brooklyn Museum, New York.

In the south, on the coast, the inhabitants could only partially escape the highly pervasive influence of Chavín. The chief centers of artistic development lay in the valleys of Nazca, Ica, and Pisco. On the arid Paracas Peninsula, to which the natives of the region brought their dead, the burial grounds give evidence of two distinct early cultures. The older one is called Paracas Cavernas, because of the caverns in which the dead were laid away, and is dated around 500 to 100 B.C. The later culture is known as Paracas Necropolis, from the Greek word for burial place, and it flourished sometime between 200 B.C. and A.D. 200. The distinctive mark of the earlier culture is its highly diversified polychrome ceramic ware, which strove for and achieved a newer style than the old forms of the Chavín Culture. The characteristic form of globular jug with a spout (right) was subjected to variation until finally a form with a double spout was devised, and this remained typical of the Nazca Culture which followed, and thereby also of pottery throughout the southern coastal region.

Upper left: Polychrome bowl decorated with a figure of a mythical creature. Baked clay, height 3⅛". Paracas Cavernas Culture, Ocucaje style, c. 500–100 B.C. From Ica Valley, southern coast of Peru. Collection Nathan Cummings, Chicago.

Lower left: Belly-shaped jar with hoop handle and spout. Baked clay, height 7¾". Paracas Cavernas Culture, Ocucaje style, c. 500–100 B.C. From Cerro Blanco, Ocucaje, southern coast of Peru. Collection Nathan Cummings, Chicago.

Lower right: Vessel in the shape of a monkey. Baked clay, height 6⅝". Paracas Cavernas Culture, Ocucaje style, c. 500–100 B.C. From Ica Valley, southern coast of Peru. Collection Nathan Cummings, Chicago.

Facing page: Detail of a large night-blue burial blanket with puma-demons embroidered in alpaca wool on cotton cloth. Dimensions of detail 35⅜ × 23⅝". Paracas Necropolis Culture, c. 200 B.C.–A.D. 200. From southern coast of Peru. Linden Museum, Stuttgart.

Perhaps the most important of the Paracas ceramics are those in Ocucaje style, named after the major archaeological site in the Ica Valley. So far, archaeologists have been able to separate out ten distinct variants in style and technique. Especially attractive are those vessels painted in strong, almost lacquerlike colors, whose decoration was applied only after the clay had been fired (upper left and lower right). In this type, the designs were first outlined by incised lines in order to prevent the colors from running into each other.

Bowl. Baked clay painted in bright colors, height 3 1/8″. Paracas Cavernas Culture, Ocucaje style, c. 500–100 B.C. From Ica Valley, southern coast of Peru. Collection Nathan Cummings, Chicago.

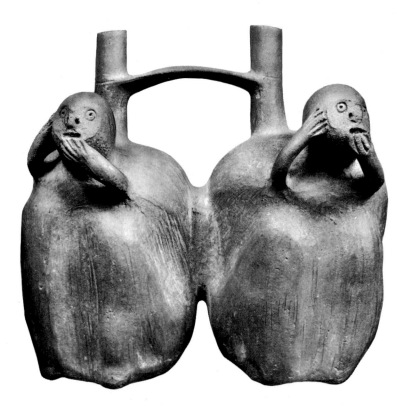

Jug in the form of two monkeys, with two tubular spouts connected by a hoop-shaped handle. Baked clay, height 5 7/8″. Paracas Necropolis Culture, c. 200 B.C.–A.D. 200. Textile Museum, Washington, D. C.

Embroidered cotton cloth. Dimensions of fragment 7⅛ × 5⅞". Paracas Necropolis Culture, c. 200 B.C.–A.D. 200. From southern coast of Peru. Private collection, Zurich.

The Paracas Necropolis Culture would scarcely have won such an important place in the history of Peruvian art if it were merely a matter of its monochromatic pottery. It owes that place entirely to its *mantas*, its mantles for the dead. The eviscerated dead bodies were wrapped like mummies in the most sumptuous cloth—something we would interpret as sheer extravagance—and then laid away on the Paracas Peninsula. Often folded blankets with embroidered designs were also laid on the breasts of the dead. These were intended to keep the deceased warm in the icy world of dead men and demons (above, also page 177).

In the dry soil, impregnated with saltpeter, of this virtually rainless zone, these products of the weavers' industriousness, with their fantastic motifs and gleaming colors intact, have survived to our time in good condition. Junius Bird of the American Museum of Natural History, New York, studied one of these death mantles which was 85′ 29¼″ long and 11′ 3″ wide. If the thread of the warp were laid out in a straight line, it would stretch 74½ miles.

Almost all the ways of weaving used today were known in that now extinct world. Something like 190 colors and shades were available to the artists to convey their prayers to the gods and demons of the other world. The dead, in their conception, were intermediaries between the living and the powers of the Beyond.

Detail of a burial blanket. Cotton embroidered with alpaca wool, dimensions of detail
7$^1/_8$ × 6$^1/_4$". Paracas Necropolis Culture, c. 200 B.C.–A.D. 200. From southern coast of Peru.
Textile Museum, Washington, D. C.

In southern Peru the belief was widespread that the victor in a battle acquired his enemy's strength and skill
by chopping off his head. The most frequent subjects in the weaving and pottery of that region are winged
creatures together with wildcats, usually holding in one hand a head as a trophy, along with serpents and
aquatic animals—creatures of the other world illustrating long forgotten myths. Like magical incantations
repeated endlessly from the most ancient times, these fantastic beings are portrayed over and over again with
a secure instinct for chromatic harmonies based on more than 190 different shades of colors which were
made from vegetable, animal, or mineral matter. The *mantas* from Paracas employ color symbolically, as do
the very much later Mixtec pictographs and the Maya books with their hieroglyphs and pictures of the gods.
But the exact meanings attributed to their colors by this preliterate society have been lost to us. The materials
used for these burial blankets were cotton, alpaca, or vicuña wool.

The cat-demons of the Paracas Necropolis burial cloths lived on for the next three or four centuries as decorations on the pottery of the Nazca Culture. Most of that decoration is supercharged with symbolic ornamentation which never gives an exact picture of the person or thing portrayed, and this has led many scholars to suspect that it may have some hieroglyphic meaning. No doubt here too the decoration had the character of magical formulas and prayers to be conveyed by the dead to the demons and gods. Certainly the many depictions of fish were connected with prayers for fertility, though more for the fields than for the family (below).

In the thin-walled, graceful, glowingly colored, and technically perfect ceramics of the southern coast, the image is transformed into a symbol. They are as different as can be from the realistic pottery of Moche on the northern coast. As for the overall forms of Nazca ceramics, they were taken over from the Paracas Culture. There is no attempt at individualization such as portrayals of princes, priests, or warriors, and all the thought behind them appears to be rooted in the world of demons and gods. It is likely that the conditions of life were less favorable in the southern coastlands than in the north. Other than the trophy heads, nothing in the pottery or weaving suggests that the Nazcas may have been a warlike people or that they had any territorial ambitions. No remains have been found of fortifications or temples of any importance.

Vessel in the form of a predatory fish with humanlike face. Polychrome painted baked clay, length c. 9″. Classic Nazca style, c. 400–600. From southern coast of Peru. Private collection.

Stirrup-handled jug with double spout, decorated with hummingbirds sipping at a flower. Painted baked clay, height 5³/₄″. Nazca Culture, c. A.D. 250–750. From southern coast of Peru. Linden Museum, Stuttgart. Sutorius Collection.

Stirrup-handled jug with double spout, ▶ decorated with a puma-demon coiling around the body of the vessel, wearing a golden mouth mask and holding a trophy head. Polychrome painted baked clay, height 6¹/₄″. Nazca Culture, c. A.D. 250–750. From southern coast of Peru. Private collection, Washington, D. C.

Two vessels in the form of demons decorated with budding plants. Polychrome painted baked clay, height 5¹/₂″. Nazca Culture, c. A.D. 250–750. From southern coast of Peru. Private collection, Washington, D. C.

In Nazca ceramics, spatial depth is no more than an intellectual concept: everything in the style is concerned with surface design. Not until the late phase did potters work in sculptural forms such as those on the next two pages. Their pottery painting falls into two main groups. In the first, in spite of stylization, one easily recognizes motifs such as birds, fish, and plants, which serve as fertility symbols (facing page, above). The second group consists of purely religious mythical subjects. The feline gods of Chavín and Paracas wear large golden masks over their mouths, as did the priests, to show that their primitive wildness has been tamed, and only the trophy heads they hold recall the bloody sacrifices made to them. The ornaments which surround them are usually sprouting plants.

Fertility and death are the central concerns of most primitive religions, but perhaps nowhere more so than in Nazca, which carried on the tradition of Paracas. The fertility cult took on special importance where there was an unceasing struggle for a few precious drops of water and against the all-destroying sun, as in the river valleys of the southern coast, the only oases in the midst of those desert wastes. Only the political union with other, more productive agricultural regions which took place in later times relieved these people from their obsessive concern with sources of food, and turned their exclusively religious orientation to other directions. That social change is clearly reflected in their crafts. The subtle pottery painting of the Nazcas was never again matched in later years, and in later cultures of the southern coast even the old handicraft techniques declined.

Jug in the form of a musician with ▶
panpipes, drum, and horn held up
like an ear-trumpet. Polychrome
painted baked clay, height $7^1/_2$".
Nazca Culture, c. 250–750. From
southern coast of Peru. Private
collection, Buenos Aires.

Vessel in form of three vegetables,
probably chili pepper pods. Painted
baked clay, height $4^3/_4$". Nazca Culture, c. 250–750. From southern
coast of Peru. Private collection,
Washington, D. C.

The most successful people in the world in the cultivation of useful plants were the Indians. More than half
the agricultural products used today were cultivated by them, including maize, the chief food of the Americas
and the second in importance in the world. The most important vegetable for Europe, the potato, came from
the New World, as did beans, cocoa, tobacco, tomatoes, pumpkins, chili peppers, vanilla, quinine, coca, and
many other plants. But above all it was maize that put an end to the hunters' nomadic way of life and made
possible a settled home for the Indians.

The artists of the Nazca Culture did not neglect food plants as motifs for their pottery decoration. Much of it
is based on a motif of sprouting plants, and in the late phases plants even gave rise to sculptural forms such
as the vessel in vegetable shape seen above. In the culture flourishing at the same time in Moche on the northern
coast, men and everyday objects were portrayed in clay, but in the south almost nothing has been found except
depictions of demons or, occasionally, musicians, though the latter were probably priests. That the musician
seen here may be a priest is suggested by the serpents dangling from the neck of the vessel. Here too we
see the two instruments which are still the favorites of the Indians in Peru and Bolivia, the panpipes and skin
drum.

Vessel with stirrup-ring spout, decorated with a priest performing a ritual beneath a starry sky. Baked clay painted in reddish brown over a whitish ground, height $9^1/_2''$. Moche Culture, c. 200–800. From northern coast of Peru. Linden Museum, Stuttgart.

Ritual mask in the form of a puma head flanked by condors, probably part of a headdress. Cold-hammered thin gold sheet, $9^1/_4 \times 10^1/_4''$. Early phase of Moche Culture, c. 200–400. From northern coast of Peru. André Emmerich Gallery, New York.

The epoch in which the realistic art of Moche and the stylizations of Nazca reached their highest point is known as their classic age or the period of the skilled craftsmen. Several hundred miles of semidesert separate the centers of these two almost contemporary cultures, and it is not surprising that they developed in fundamentally opposite directions. And yet, both Moche and Nazca shared the lot of all the Peruvian cultures on the coast: despite the high level of development attained, they remained strictly local. This was due not to geography alone but also, obviously, to the undynamic mentality of the coastal peoples.

Pottery was the chief means of expression of all early Peruvians. That of Moche portrays the world of men but, at the same time, seeks to conjure up the other world. This people, of whom we know no more than the name of one of their sites, devised for itself a world picture of rather more unassuming character. The solemn and fanatical aspects of Chavín made way here for a happier, more earthy attitude toward life. Even priests became more worldly, more accessible to public view. They are depicted at the hunt or in games or practicing their rites (facing page). The gods themselves stepped down from their remote heights to become no more than scary animal faces or masks behind which there was a man and which served only to adorn the head of a priest (above).

Vessel in the form of a water bird. Baked clay with brownish painting on a light ground, height 7⁷/₈″. Moche Culture, c. 200–800. From Chicama Valley, northern coast of Peru. Linden Museum, Stuttgart.

What has been called the "ceramic library," as distinct from pottery for everyday use, is comprised of three basic types. In the first, globular vessels are decorated with painted scenes. In the second, painted decoration is replaced by relief modeling. The third type is made up of fully three-dimensional sculptures in which only the stirrup-ring spout, which remained typical of all vessels on the northern coast, reminds us that this is really a utensil (above). With this form a technical difficulty was solved: how to preserve the necessary hollow space inside during the firing process and thereby prevent the vessel from bursting apart. Because of its fidelity to reality, its skillful craftsmanship, and its artistic execution, the local culture of Moche has become one of the best known in all of South America.

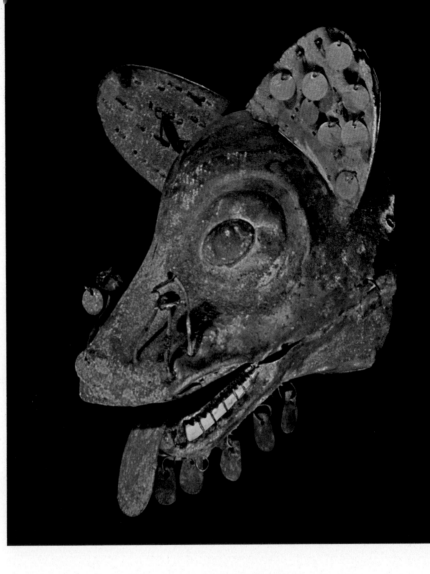

Head of a fox or coyote. Alloy of gold, copper, and silver, cold-hammered and assembled from separate pieces, with teeth of mussel shell, length 5⅞″. Moche Culture, c. 200–800. From the Moon Pyramid in Moche, northern coast of Peru. Linden Museum, Stuttgart.

According to the Spanish chronicler Calancha, in the time immediately after the Conquest gold worth something more than 80,000 pesos was removed and melted down from the Sun Pyramid of Moche alone. Yet of even greater importance was the pyramid dedicated to the moon, the "Huaca de la Luna," the holiest place of the Moche Culture. The spiritual bond linking all the coast peoples was, in fact, moon worship. This head of a fox or coyote came from that sacred pyramid. In the north, the fox and the owl were lunar symbols since both are creatures of the night, whereas in the south it was the puma-god who was associated with the moon (in Mediterranean cultures, the cat was considered the mother of the moon). Only in the highlands was the heat-dispensing sun revered.

It was particularly in metalwork that the Moche Culture made important innovations. Although goldsmithing had been known as far back as the Chavín Culture, now work in silver, copper, and lead as well as the lost-wax (*cire perdue*) method of casting came to enrich the technical possibilities. Bronze was still unknown, but a copper and silver alloy of gold was devised and used, as in the object pictured here.

Vessel in the form of a portrait head of a high-placed personality, either a priest or a prince. Baked clay painted in light and dark brown, height 11 3/8″. Late Moche Culture, c. 400–800. From northern coast of Peru. Linden Museum, Stuttgart.

Top part of a sword showing a jaguar attacking a naked man, perhaps a prisoner offered in sacrifice. Solid algarroba wood with mother-of-pearl inlay, height of the figures 7″. Late Moche Culture, c. 400–800. From northern coast of Peru. Textile Museum, Washington, D. C.

The Moche Culture reached a high point in depiction of the human countenance in its portrait vessels, which are characterized by an accurate grasp of reality and superb individualization. The distinction between various types of physiognomy is no less than astonishing. There are symmetrically formed heads which even to European tastes are handsome, but also faces distorted by illness or human passions. Indeed, human weaknesses, even physical handicaps, seem to have inspired the artists as much as the pure beauty of a face. With the simplest of means, as for instance the deft shaping of the eyes, utterly lifelike effects are achieved, whether what is aimed at is haughty pride or terror (above). Pride and calm musing speak from the eyes of princes (facing page), grim wrath from those of the gods and their warriors, submission from those of the naked seated prisoners, and fatigue and exhaustion from those of workers. Always it is the gaze, the "Mochica gaze," which is the main factor in the expressive power of these portraits.

No attempt was ever made in Moche pottery to render perspective. Every important element was depicted from its most impressive angle: the face always in profile, the crescent-shaped headdress and garments in front view. Overlapping of figures or objects was painstakingly avoided. What is most seductive in these vase paintings is the rhythmic movement and subtle feeling for form, along with the harmonious contrast of reddish brown colors overlaying a whitish background. Compared to Moche works in sculpture, their painted scenes are less naturalistic. They concern chiefly gods or priests, and here, too, trophy heads are frequent, though not in connection with demons or gods as in the Nazca Culture, but instead, with priests, who are the gods' representatives on earth and are always clearly presented as human beings (facing page).

Warrior with club and round shield. Baked clay, height 8″. Late Moche Culture, c. 400–800. From northern coast of Peru. British Museum, London.

Certainly the Moche were not a peaceful folk. Had they been, there would have been no reason to commemorate warriors armed with shield and club on so many vessels (facing page) and in so many statues (above). Even prisoners found a place on these ceramics. Naked, a rope around their neck and loins as a sign of subjugation, they await their doom, which meant being thrown off a precipice after being judged by a priest in the mask and costume of the god to whom the victim would be sacrificed (right).

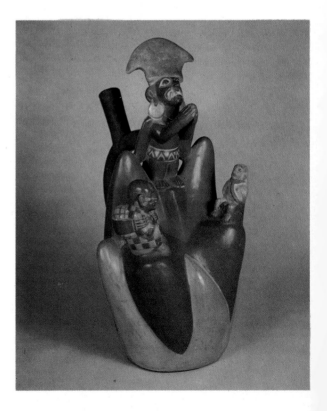

Vessel with figures: In a stylized mountainous landscape a demon, or a priest wearing the mask of a god, passes judgment on a seated bound naked prisoner. Painted baked clay, height 11³/₄″. Late Moche Culture, c. 400–800. From northern coast of Peru. Museum of the American Indian, Heye Foundation, New York.

Jug with stirrup-ring spout decorated with an animal-demon warrior holding a war ax and a trophy head. Painted baked clay, height 8″. Moche Culture, c. 200–800. From Chimbote, northern coast of Peru. Linden Museum, Stuttgart. Sutorius Collection.

The Sun Gate of Tiahuanaco. Height c. 9′ 10″. Classic Tiahuanaco Culture, c. 300–600. Tiahuanaco, Bolivia.

Detail of a textile with ▶ highly stylized figures of gods. Dimensions of detail 27 1/2 × 19 5/8″. Late classic Tiahuanaco Culture, c. 500–700. Provenance unknown. Brooklyn Museum, New York.

What is identified as the Sun Gate at Tiahuanaco is neither as large nor as imposing as other monuments of the extinct Indian civilizations. It makes its impact only when we examine its frieze, which is almost twelve feet long and three feet high. In the middle stands the central divinity, the sun-god. To either side are three rows of winged, armed demons, all hastening toward the center. Those of the top and bottom tiers have human faces, those in the middle have bird heads or bird masks. The sun, the condor, and the jaguar embody the fundamental ideas which the Tiahuanaco style pitted against the lunar conception of the world held by the coast peoples. Once again, as had happened in the Chavín Culture, the lowland people succumbed to the religious fanaticism of the highlanders. The influence spread from Tiahuanaco, first to the decadent Nazca Culture of the coast, and then gradually also to the north. As a result, the effects of this influence from the southern highlands can be traced in almost every local culture of the coastland for at least two centuries.

The site of the ruins of Tiahuanaco, which gave its name to this culture and is among the most impressive of early South America, lies in the vicinity of Lake Titicaca. But, alas, the past tense is more appropriate here, because for centuries the residents of this region have taken stones from its buildings to be used for their own. Such spoliation has made even more obscure this great and mysterious culture, whose beginnings are as unknown to us as those of Chavín. And yet, when one stands in this complex of ruins lying over 13,000 feet above sea level, one senses that this must have been the spiritual center of a mighty kingdom. Many of its religious edifices are unfinished and convey the impression that their builders simply abandoned them halfway, though so far no grounds for this belief have been found. Heyerdahl's hypothesis that the people who settled the Polynesian islands came from here presupposes that there was an emigration consequent upon a collapse of theocratic power, but concrete evidence for this is lacking.

The finest hand-woven textiles ever made were turned out by the Tiahuanaco people. In contrast to the Chavín style, that of Tiahuanaco is angular and squared-off, without loops or curves. All natural forms were deliberately converted into geometrical forms. In textiles especially one is reminded of Cubist painting (facing page). The religious conceptions of this people banned all imitation of nature. The jaguar is rarely depicted as a jaguar, and when it appears it is generally combined with condor heads. In textile patterns it is so transformed into shapes as to be almost unrecognizable. What impelled this people to reduce their picture of nature to these abstract, purely geometrical forms, to something intellectual and artificial, is something we can only conjecture. Probably it was felt that the divine should not assume the profane forms of the world of humans.

Figure, probably, because of the elaborate face painting, a priest or prince, Polychrome painted baked clay, height 12¹/₄″. Epigonal Tiahuanaco Culture, c. 500–800. From Necropolis of Anja, upper Montaro Valley, Huancayo Province, Peru. Rietberg Museum, Zurich.

Facing page: Detail of a textile with highly stylized jaguar-figure pattern. Tapestry technique, natural vicuña-color background with red strips and patterns in black, rose, turquoise, and in various shades of red and brown, c.41 × 43″ (double-faced). Late classic Tiahuanaco Culture, c. 500–700. Provenance unknown. Textile Museum, Washington, D.C.

Incense burner with fully modeled puma head. Polychrome painted baked clay, height 11³/₄″. Classic Tiahuanaco Culture, c. 300–600. Probably from vicinity of Lake Titicaca. Collection Fritz Buck, La Paz, Bolivia.

Vessel in the form of a serpent, decorated with heads of gods and magical signs. Painted baked clay, height 9⅞". Epigonal Tiahuanaco style, c. 500–800. Probably from central coastal region. Museum of the American Indian, Heye Foundation, New York.

At the outset, the classic Tiahuanaco style does not appear to have spread over any large area. Later, however, its stylistic traits and figurations of the gods became the main stock of the entire Central Andes region. The central coastland proved a particularly fertile and still vital terrain for the Tiahuanaco Culture. From the textile designs of this period we can see that the old, long-established forms of the gods and their rites had to give way to the new ones from the highlands. On ornaments made of shell, often inlaid with precious metals and semiprecious stones, we meet again, as on textiles and ceramics, the motifs used on the Sun Gate (left). Under the influence of the new style the Moche Culture of the northern coast, which by that time was already in decline, simply collapsed without resistance. No direct evidence in the form of art or any other has survived to tell of the end of its priests and princes. But that the cultural decline and collapse must have gone to the very roots of this society is shown by the fact that the usually exhaustive chronicles breathe not a single word about such a decisive social change. All that we can learn from the grave offerings is that the differences between religious and everyday pottery tended to disappear.

In the course of the centuries, the population in the various parts of the land increased. Separatist tendencies developed in these groups, and finally led to the leveling-out of the originally sharply structured religious unity of the sun cult, and therewith also to the weakening of the political and economic cohesion of the different tribes. When Tiahuanaco declined as a religious center, the fountainhead of that culture and the active impulses behind it dried up. Nevertheless, it was not until the tenth century that the outworn style gradually disappeared.

Deity flanked by two demon faces and holding serpent wands. Shell (*Spondylus pictorum*) inlaid with pieces of shell of other colors. Epigonal Tiahuanaco style, c. 500–800. Probably from central coastal region. Private collection, Zurich.

Bowl with drinking scene in full modeling on base. Black baked clay, height 8³/₄". Chimu Culture, c. 1200–1463. From Santa Valley, northern coast of Peru. Formerly private collection, Basel.

The historical period that began then is known as that of the City Builders. The exponents of this culture, the Chimu people, were highly successful in politics, but in art they never attained even the level of the Moche Culture. They pushed the frontiers of their land some 560 miles farther north. Their well-organized state, with around 250,000 inhabitants in the capital, Chan Chan, was the first to justify calling this the City Builders period. Nowhere else in South America was their competence in urban organization equaled, and their roads across the trackless wastelands preceded the world-famous ones built by the Incas. Chan Chan covered an area of almost seven square miles. Like other chief cities of the time, it lay somewhat outside the fertile river valleys, in order not to squander arable land on building. It contained huge pyramids, nothing comparable to those of Mexico and Central America, and there were temples and blocks of dwellings lined up in close proximity to each other but separated by fountains and well-watered gardens. All of this indicates that Chan Chan was the greatest trading center on the northern coast. The arts and crafts of the Chimu Culture are lacking in the fantasy and high skill that its predecessor, the Moche Culture, possessed. The motifs used were the same: animals, princes, warriors, erotic scenes. But the execution was deficient in artistic subtlety and technical skill. The object pictured here is, in fact, above the average in quality.

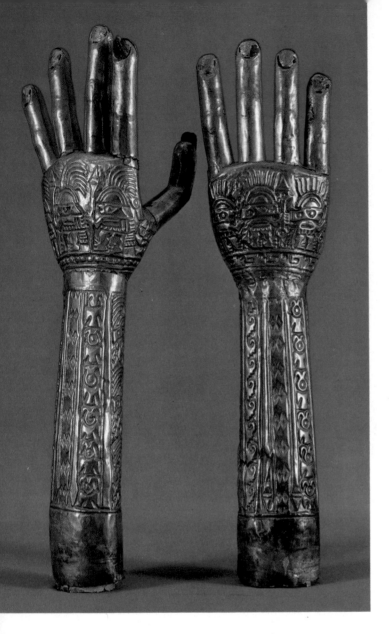

Large death mask. Alloy of gold and silver with ▶
copper pieces added and vestiges of original painting,
$9^1/_2 \times 15^3/_4$". Chimu Culture, c. 1200–1463. From
northern coast of Peru. Stolper Galleries, Munich.

Funerary gloves decorated with small idols embossed
on the back of the hands and zoomorphic motifs on
the forearms. Lenght $21^7/_8$", width $7^7/_8$". Chimu
Culture, c. 1200–1463.

The capital of the Chimu kingdom lies in ruins, like the other cities where men once lived and worshiped. The
Chimus were the most redoubtable foes of the Incas and were not subjugated until around the middle of the
fifteenth century. According to the old Spanish chronicles, even this would not have been possible had not
the Incas quite literally drained away the water supply of the Chimu highlands and diverted it into the desert
region. Today Chan Chan lies almost entirely buried under the drifting sands of the coast, though parts of the
city have been exposed by the rains.

Although the Chimu Culture achieved no advance over what others had done in pottery and weaving,
it did make notable improvements in the third branch of handicrafts, metallurgy. The large number of sur-

viving bowls, drinking vessels, masks, and ornaments, mostly in gold or silver and either cold-hammered or cast, suggests that there must have been a veritable industry producing such objects. Evidence for this is not lacking. The chronicler Calancha tells of 6,000 Indians who toiled in gold, silver, and copper mines for their king. Diggings in Chan Chan corroborate this: in one of the ten parts of the city excavated the remains of numerous forges were found. The Chimus were acquainted not only with all the techniques of casting and plating gold, but also with work in bronze. Their skill in metalwork seems to have been so exceptional and so admired that the victorious Incas took away to their capital a good many Chimu specialists in that craft.

Many Chimu customs and forms of artistic expression betray their close connection with the older culture of Moche, though the Chimus themselves seem to have had no knowledge of their predecessors. According to their legends, which were written down between 1576 and 1586 by the Spaniard Miguel Cabello de Balboa, a mighty prince called Naym-Lap, with a great horde and a great flotilla, landed on the Chimu coast at a time so remote in the past that they had no way even of speaking of it. Along with his consort and many other women, he brought also his royal trumpeter, cupbearer, master of ceremonies, cook, tailor, bath attendant, and the man whose task it was to paint his face. Not only did he bring all his court and staff, says the legend, but also his own palace, entire and fully decorated.

Vessel in the form of the head of an old man. Baked clay with reddish painting, height 8¹/₄″. Chimu Culture, c. 1200–1463. From northern coast of Peru. British Museum, London.

Part of a cotton fabric woven in various techniques, among them openwork, with a pattern of birds whose tail feathers are in the style of the period of Inca domination. Fifteenth century. From central coastal region of Peru.

The grave offerings of the Chimus were like those of other cultures: foodstuffs, tools, pottery, textiles. The vessels often give the impression of objects turned out by mass production. When there are figures, they lack any individualistic traits and even any expression of joy or sorrow. Only in the weaving, in the glow of its colors and the variety of its motifs, is there any connection with the preceding epoch, that of the coastal Tiahuanacos, themselves late followers of a great tradition. True, the motifs have changed: now they are mostly stylized fish and birds, the symbols of fertility (facing page). Neither the jaguar of the highlands nor the puma of the southern coast appears now. There is, however, one characteristic motif which distinguishes northern coast textiles, a breaking-wave pattern used as an ornamental border.

Artistic products without religious significance were virtually unknown to the peoples of early America. None of the several American languages has a word for art or artist, though—as single exception—the Zapotecs in Mexico do have one which roughly approximates our term "art."

Egg-shaped jug with spout depicting a man and a puma. Gray-violet painting on a whitish ground, crude baked clay, height 12⅝″. Chancay Culture, c. 1200–1500. From central coast of Peru. Private collection, Zurich.

Loose-woven fabric with stylized figure of a man. Height of fragment 15″. Pachacamac Culture, after 1000. From central coast of Peru. Museum für Völkerkunde, Munich.

On the central coast, the Tiahuanaco Culture was followed by that of Chancay, whose style seems to have forgotten all the artistic and technical achievements of the previous two hundred years. The regression is most obvious in their very naïve and crude pottery. Typically these are bulky egg-shaped jugs, usually with a spout in the form of a face. Such vessels—mistakenly called urns—lack all feeling for proportion. The range of colors in their decoration is limited to violet-gray and black, with usually no more than a soft red added.

Even today, before starting a new fabric, Peruvian weavers pray for God's blessing. There is no doubt that in Pre-Columbian times textile weaving was a religious function, especially when it was a matter of the cloths used only for wrapping the dead. A great many of the Peruvian textiles came from the central coast. There lay Pachacamac, one of the greatest and most important pilgrimage places, which even under the Incas lost little of its importance. To it came pilgrims from the north and south alike. Although that contact had no influence on pottery, it did have some effect on textile designs. In the thirteenth to fifteenth centuries there was some mutual influence and stimulation between the individual small neighboring kingdoms along the coast. But it was in the centers directly connected with Pachacamac that the artisans reacted most to ideas from abroad. The result was that the local styles, which earlier had been sharply differentiated, finally blended into a single cosmopolitan style whose individual elements it is difficult for us today to sort out.

"One day I asked my uncle about how the Empire began, and he readily gave me answer: 'Keep in your heart', he said, 'all that I tell you. You know that earlier, in the old times, the land here was desolate and empty and men lived without morals, like the wild beasts. When the sun-god, our father, beheld this, he had pity and sent down from heaven one of his sons, Manco Capac, and one of his daughters, Mama Ocllo, to be gods to those men and to teach them how to live with each other in understanding and love. From his two children men were to learn also to build houses and to till the soil and to do all the other things civilized man does.'" Thus wrote El Inca, Garcilaso de la Vega, a chronicler who traced his ancestry back to both the Inca

dynasty and the family of the great Spanish poet of the same name. The children of the sun-god were instructed to settle wherever they could plunge their staffs easily into the earth, and legend says that this was in the vicinity of Cuzco. In reality, however, as early as the middle of the thirteenth century a ruling caste had grown out of the tribe of the Quechuas in this very isolated region, and it was they who became the Incas. Properly speaking, the Incas were neither a tribe nor a race: Inca is no more than the name of a dynasty. Their influence quickly made itself felt. They gave a new impulse to the sun cult of the highlands, since the chief of the Incas claimed to be born directly of the sun-god. All important posts were kept in the family and handed down from father to son. At the top of the social pyramid was enthroned the Inca himself, the single, all-powerful ruler.

Textile with a pattern of figures, some in profile, some frontal, but with faces always seen frontally. 16⁷/₈ × 17³/₈". Chancay Culture, c. 1200–1500. From central coast of Peru. Private collection, Zurich.

Crowned god (Naym-Lap). Solid gold set with precious stones, 15³/₄ × 8¹/₄". From the region of Illimo, Lambayeque, Peru. Collection Miguel Mujica Gallo, Peru.

Featherwork, probably a ceremonial standard. Feathers of exotic birds on cotton, height 19⅝". Inca Culture, c. 1350–1532. From southern coast of Peru. Private collection, Zurich.

Poncho with design of pumas in red. Featherwork, 23⅝ × 25⅝". Inca ▶ Culture, c. 1350–1532. Probably from central highlands or southern coast of Peru. Linden Museum, Stuttgart.

Beaker of *keru* type with carved animal figures as handles and painted decoration showing a procession. Carved and painted wood, height 7⅞". Early colonial period, c. 1532–1570. From southern or central highlands of Peru. Textile Museum, Washington, D. C.

The Inca ruling caste surpassed all of its predecessors in imposing its will on the various Indian tribes. With Machiavellian subtlety it exploited the deeply rooted mythological lore of the Indians to serve its own overweening expansionist policy. With the help of its powerful military forces and an equally well-organized hierarchy of officials, the Inca empire finally controlled an area covering thirty-seven degrees of latitude. A major part of its culture was based on the already existing achievements of the peoples it subjugated and on those of earlier cultures, and in this the Incas were very like the Aztecs.

It was only in the heart of their territory that a true Inca style developed. In other places the crafts were influenced by local customs, as was the case with religion also. But the concept of a unified state promoted by the founders of the empire was not without an effect on the arts: the Inca style put an end to individualistic creativity. The personal audacity of the earlier artists was crushed by rigorous control, and only much later did it again find an outlet for imaginative creation—in painting the heavy wooden drinking vessels called *kerus* (right).

"In my kingdom no bird flies, no leaf quivers if I do not will it"—these words that the Inca Atahuallpa flung in the face of the Spaniard Pizarro are the perfect illustration of the ostentation with which the "Son of the God" bore his certainty of power. As head of the dynasty and the state, and as a self-proclaimed divinity, he could command absolute obedience from his subjects. Any misdemeanor anywhere in his empire could be interpreted as an offence against the Inca himself, and therefore against God, and severely punished.

In the Inca Culture, it is in objects destined for the aristocracy that we find a certain artistic freedom combined with a high level of craftsmanship. The costumes of European kings and emperors were in no way more sumptuous than the ceremonial robes of the Inca overlords, which were made by their concubines, or those of the Inca himself, which—at least according to the Spanish chroniclers—were created by the Virgins of the Sun. A very special type of these included outer garments made of the varicolored feathers of exotic birds.

Nowhere is the impression of the despotic power wielded by the Inca rulers more striking than in their architecture. Quite unlike the practice in Mexico, the Incas were indifferent to splendidly colored ornamental façades, though their rooms were magnificently furnished with superb hangings and decorations in precious metals. The starkly bare exterior walls were constructed from huge squared-off blocks of stone, many of them weighing several tons, which were so closely set one on the other that only rarely can a knife blade be inserted between them. There is no decoration, and nothing enlivens the walls except the different sizes of the stone blocks. No mortar or other binding material was used, but the joining is so perfect that many walls have through the ages withstood the earthquakes which are so frequent in this region and which, time and again, have toppled the churches the conquerors later built on the foundations of old structures. It is said that 50,000 Indians worked more than twenty years to build the capital city, and for the fortress of Sacsayhuaman (below), which protects Cuzco by a system of elevated trenches laid out in zigzag formation, the Spanish chroniclers report that 30,000 workers were required during eight years. Such reports do not seem at all exaggerated when we look at the lower walls of the formerly three-story ramparts which have defiantly withstood all the ravages of time. "Now that the lords of the Incas have lost their power, all those palaces and dwellings, along with their other great constructions, have fallen into ruin, and no more than vestiges of their architecture remain. But they were built of solid stone, and the masonry was so expertly done that they will stand for centuries as their memorials"—when Pedro de Cieza de León wrote these lines in mid-sixteenth century he proved himself a true prophet.

Trapezoid gateway at head of staircase. Inca Culture, fifteenth century. Sacsayhuaman, southern highlands of Peru, above Cuzco.

Cyclopean walls of the Fortress of Sacsayhuaman. Inca Culture, c. 1450. Southern highlands of Peru, above Cuzco.

After the murder of the last Inca ruler, Atahuallpa, on August 29, 1533, the Spanish conquerors remained the undisputed masters of the country. The defeated people were a flock without a shepherd, and scarcely understood what had happened to them. True, the Spaniards promised the eldest surviving son of Huayna Capac, a nephew of Atahuallpa, that the kingdom would be rebuilt. But as the years passed they made not the slightest move in that direction, so that at last he attempted to organize an insurrection. This came to nought, and so he assembled all the men of his blood, sent his faithful warriors back to their homelands, and himself chose exile in the trackless wastes of the mountains. But he too was to meet his fate at the hands of the Spaniards: he was killed in 1545 in a quarrel with a deserter to whom he had offered refuge. The last asylum of the Inca Culture was the city to which he had retreated, Machu Picchu in the Urubamba Valley.

Machu Picchu spreads out majestic and beautiful in its mountain setting in the central Andes. What men built there gave pride of place to nature. None of the Spanish conquerors ever discovered the last hiding place of the Inca nobles, and there is not a word of it in the accounts of the chroniclers and colonial officials. Not until 1911 did the American archaeologist Hiram Bingham discover this hidden mountain fortress, which lies only forty-two miles from Cuzco, the "Navel-of-the-World," as the Incas called their capital city. How long Machu Picchu continued to be inhabited after the Spanish Conquest remains a mystery buried with the Incas.

PART TWO:

LATER INDIAN TRIBAL ARTS

TEXT BY FREDERICK J. DOCKSTADER

In assessing the aboriginal arts of the Americas it is most practical to consider the regions geographically rather than attempting to divide them by their chronological or anthropological boundaries. The reader must realize that we are discussing almost one-half of the world's area, and a tenth or so of its population; moreover, these arts are the result of some 25,000 years' development, upon which many influences have been expressed, both prehistorically and more recently. The Hemisphere is simply too vast, and the art expressions are too varied, to allow more limited and specific distinction in such a short discussion.

For these reasons it will be most convenient to travel in a north-to-south direction, following much the same route as the early Indian, who apparently entered the Americas by way of the Bering Straits, journeyed south and east, expanding subsequently into the neighboring regions of the Hemisphere. This will necessarily violate some tribal relationships and visual elements of identification, but it will permit greater consideration of Indian aesthetics as a group expression.

This section is limited to the so-called tribal arts, sometimes termed ethnic arts as part of the larger world of "primitive art"; it will include only the aboriginal aesthetic activities of America of the historic period. Actually, these arts will necessarily date from about 1850—most earlier work has long since disappeared into the oblivion of decay or loss, through both natural and man-made destruction.

Space does not allow for any specific or minute consideration of these arts and crafts, and the text will, in large part, present only comments upon the subject matter and origins of Indian arts. The bibliography appended will allow the reader an opportunity for greater reference.

The several divisions follow an arbitrary delimitation, not so much for anthropological accuracy as for a similarity in the use of natural environment and the equally important diversity of artistic expression. Thus, the fact that many tribes in a given region make much the same objects following a similar design pattern is no more vital to an understanding of ethnic art than is the fact that just as often one encounters regions wherein tribes have almost nothing in common in those artistic efforts.

ARCTIC AMERICA. In the far North, adjoining and including the Arctic Circle, the Eskimo have long established a healthy relationship with their environment. Late-comers insofar as many of the other tribal peoples are concerned, the Eskimo have nevertheless adjusted well to a relatively harsh region, and in it have found much of beauty. In art terms, most of this work is in sculpture; the use of driftwood and ivory is world-famed. The ceremonial life of the western Eskimo is important not only for providing spiritual and psychological comfort, but also assures success in the hunt, while at the same time offering protection from the hazards which threaten their everyday life. The use of a wide variety of masks, usually made from wood and ornamented with the feathers of birds and pastel paint, is widespread. Such a mask is worn by dancers who impersonate many of the spirit beings who inhabit the Eskimo world (see page 220). These dances are not as elaborate as those found farther to the south, but they exert a powerful effect upon the spectators. There is usually a strong overtone of humor in Eskimo art and ritual; this is clearly evident in the designs upon their masks.

The abundance of walrus and whale ivory permits the development of ivory carving in great numbers—in the pieces pictured on page 221 the natural forms with which the Eskimo are so familiar provide suitable models. Their artistry is impressive in its ability to make much from very little, and the remarkable mechanical skills of these folk are evident in the carved ivory and wood toggles, links, harpoon heads, and other functional articles; these have become standard over the centuries. Usually these parts are fitted into a whole in a manner which creates masterful art compositions. Designs, basically linear, include dot-and-circle motifs, abstract or realistic illustration, engraved or painted upon a surface; the lines are filled in with carbon for contrast. Rarely is perfect symmetry employed; more frequently a preference for occult balance is expressed in carving.

NORTHWEST COAST. Farther south, the people of Alaska and British Columbia, whose art embodies the greatest sculptural achievements of the North American continent, have produced an almost endless profusion of great art. Expressed in wood, bone, metal, ivory, and textiles, these creations are often inlaid with shell or metal and painted in strong designs. At their best, they become magnificent display ornaments (see page 222), primarily used to emphasize the wealth or social importance of their owners. To assure a supply of these objects, artists were maintained by wealthy patrons; indeed, this is one of the few Amerindian regions where true professional artists existed. They worked for pay, and often "belonged" to locally powerful chiefs, who absorbed their entire output.

The use of a great range of masks in ceremonies, both for the usual religious needs and for social control or prestige, is well known; often these portray legendary personages (see page 224), or they may represent mythological beings. In the more elaborate types of masks, the performer may increase the dramatic effect by the use of strings so attached as to make the masks move at will (see page 227).

Ivory, whose basic beauty the Indian readily realized, was regarded as a precious material and carved in a variety of forms; sometimes color was rubbed into the designs for greater contrast. The finished products were most often used as ornaments or charms, attached to the costume of a chief or shaman (see page 228).

Perhaps the most famous creations of this region were the great carved and painted totem poles, some extending to 70 or 80 feet in height (see page 226). Most of these do not antedate 1825 or so, even though they represent an art with a long history. Their heyday was the period following the introduction of metal tools, even though earlier examples were created by means of stone—even jade—implements. This artistry remains the most impressive of North American Indian achievements in aesthetics; the combination of a narrative, historical, and genealogical record with such sculptural pre-eminence has rarely been equaled. The rich supply of tall, straight trees whose wood was readily carved shows how quickly a people can develop an art form to take advantage of a resource.

The Northwest Coast was not limited solely to carving. Large flocks of mountain sheep and goats made available a quantity of thick woolly hair, which was harvested, spun, and woven into garments and objects of many types. The shirt depicted on page 223 not only shows off the weaver's skill, but also demonstrates the intricate designs for which this area is so noted.

Farther to the south, in areas equally luxurious in forest growth, lived the Indians of Oregon and California. The major arts found in this region had their inspiration in the heavy undergrowth of grasses and brush, which made fine basketry possible, resulting in some of the loveliest woven containers in the world (see page 229). A tremendous range of design and style is encountered here—some so divergent as to make identification immediately obvious, others so subtly different as to make concrete identification impossible.

THE PLAINS. As the Pacific area was developing, other migrants were wandering out onto the great western Plains, to come into their own Golden Age with the arrival of horses. Although we know that Indians lived in this region in prehistoric times, they seem not to have been a dominant force until the horse gave them a mobility, military strength, and economic support upon which cultural development could be based. The combination of native talent and the availability of trade objects made possible the design of such attractive garments as the magnificent man's shirt on page 231, or the smaller tobacco bag on page 230. Color was no stranger to the Plains artist; earth pigments were effective until the introduction of stronger powdered substances brought in by traders; the buffalo hide on page 232 served as the artist's canvas, upon which many designs were painted, by both men and women.

Although sculpture is found in smaller objects, such as wooden bowls, effigies, and implements (see page 230), the great sculptural art of the Northwest Coast never had as wide an outlet here, owing largely to the absence of any forest growth sufficient to make such production possible.

THE WOODLANDS. Farther east, the Indian turned to the forest for most of his artistic endeavors. The Iroquois used this material to create a corpus of mask designs representing mythological spirits (see page 238). The famous "ball-headed club" so familiar to early travelers in the East, is a true work of art, beautifully formed and balanced (page 237); this is only one of a variety of club designs favored by the Woodlands warrior. Colorful contrast was obtained by the inlaying of small bits of shell and shell beads. This interest in making the most of natural resources is demonstrated in leather work, for not only did the Indian apply a variety of substances to the surface of the hide, but he also dyed the material itself (see page 236).

One art unique to the Indian, and known nowhere else in the world, is the use of porcupine and bird quills to achieve strong design motifs. These were dyed and softened for attachment to the surface of hide objects (see page 236). Often combined with shell or, later, trade beads, these gave the costumes and implements of the Plains and Woodlands Indian great color contrast.

Indeed, the magnificent visual effects achieved by these aboriginal artists must be seen in the field to be best valued; early travelers into North America were impressed by the costumery, concerning which they wrote in great detail. Unfortunately, this was not accompanied by an equal respect for the cultures which gave birth to the arts, and little has survived; we have only tantalizing glimpses of an era now completely gone.

Another unusual material frequently used for decorative purposes is elm bark. Usually this was employed in the manufacture of containers (see page 233), in which the surface was scraped away to reveal a contrasting under-layer. The technique is found throughout the East and North, extending up into Labrador and Newfoundland, and carries over from smaller objects to the great bark canoes of the Northeast.

An early art was the use of shell beads applied to leather hides and textiles; later, as the White man brought glass beads and trade cloth, a similar technique was favored, resulting in much the same effect. The scrollwork belt is just such an example (see page 235), and the introduction of silk ribbons by settlers allowed the production of such colorful garments as the shawl on page 234.

THE SOUTHWEST. The one area in North America where ethnic arts are still a vibrant force is the south-western portion of the United States, most particularly Arizona and New Mexico. Here, almost every native art once known to have been common is still continued, although it must be admitted that the total production quantity is far less than once obtained. With increased technological skill, many of these arts are actually better made today than formerly, although they are not always as well designed; technology has a way of emphasizing skill to the detriment of talent and taste.

In ancient times, weaving made use of native cotton; the introduction of sheep made possible the manufacture of woolen textiles. The Navajo people have made perhaps the greatest achievements in this art; their textiles range in color, design, and variety of weave from the thick, heavy rug to tightly spun and woven blankets of astonishing fineness. The classic "chief's blanket" pattern on page 241 is typical; in such textiles they have even surpassed the Pueblo weavers, from whom they learned the art. Another example of Navajo adaptation is the silver necklace on page 242. This art, which they mastered in the mid-nineteenth century by watching Mexican iron workers, has become today a basic craft and economic standby for which they are world famous.

Basketry is an active craft primarily among the Hopi, Apache, and Papago people today, although formerly many other tribes, particularly the Pima, produced excellent weaves. Yet this was never as outstanding an art in the Southwest as it became in California (see pages 242–43); the more impressive accomplishment was, and remains, in the area of pottery, where a truly notable tradition can be traced far back into prehistoric times (see pages 246–47). It shares an applied-decoration approach with the ubiquitous *Kachina* doll, beloved of tourists and collectors throughout the world (see pages 244–45).

All of the Southwestern arts show a wealth of vibrancy, life, and color expressed in a wholly individual manner, and most of them have a long tradition behind them, usually extending into prehistory. Of those whose major activity seems more recent in development is the contemporary watercolor painting school represented on page 248. Although painting is known to have been practiced in ancient times, such works owe most of their present importance to the presence of non-Indian teachers, whose influence in Indian school art classes provided a major stimulus.

MEXICO AND CENTRAL AMERICA. As one goes farther south, a quite different tradition can be detected in the work of the Indian artist. The *Pascola* mask on page 249 has centuries of usage behind it, yet the inclusion of obviously European motifs, and the Christian elements apparent in the dances in which it is used, show the problem at once. All through the Latin American regions one finds European influences at work; these vary greatly from one area to another, but they keep showing up to confuse the student. Even in such relatively "pure" art expressions as weaving—certainly one which has a tremendously long period of prehistoric development—techniques or minor art motifs often betray an alien influence. The *huipil* on page 250 has prehistoric Maya counterparts, but the inclusion of non-Indian elements is detectable; ancient clay figurines demonstrate the antiquity of the design and style, even though materials used today are of alien origin.

In the Isthmus, where people were subjected to constant influences—north and south as well as east and west—one finds today an involvement of so many cultural expressions that it is almost hopeless to trace them to their basic origins. Ancient pottery designs fuse with those from the north, resulting in new, individual styles, while contemporary art forms become involved with alien motifs, both Indian and non-Indian. Out of this chronological and cultural mixture has come a series of art styles identifiable as being from this central region, yet at the same time betraying a wide variety of elements from neighboring areas. The *mola* on page 251, although reflecting an indigenous function and design, includes technical and design motifs distinctly European.

On the other hand, though the figurine on page 252 presents a purely European costume, this is a continuation of an ancient practice of carving such effigies for use in curing ceremonies. The prototype for this particular form was William Paterson, a Scotsman who set up a short-lived Utopian colony in Panama.

SOUTH AMERICA. The cultural penetration of this region by Europeans is more evident along the coastal and fringe areas than in the interior of the continent. Such ornamentation as shown on page 253 is more affected by natural resources than by human intrusion. The more creative use of nature is seen at its maximum in interior Brazil and neighboring Peru and Ecuador (see pages 254, 256). Many of the motifs and forms created in these regions can be traced to an archaeological period, but it is quite true that real "origin" usually defies isolation. Basically, most of these are simple forms which grew more complex as technology became more refined. Sometimes these differ strongly from their prehistoric predecessor, as on page 257—yet even in such cases they tend to retain an Indian flavor which allows one to suggest a distinction between Indian art and "folk art."

Regrettably, any survey of such abbreviated nature must consider only a few of the arts of the indigenous American; such expressions as body tattooing, face painting, and the wide use of casual body ornamentation cannot readily be shown—and the even more important arts of music, the dance, and literature are completely left out. And these are not minor arts, for in such highly developed cultural expressions many tribes spend a major portion of their time. It is not enough simply to create a costume, lovely though it may be; of equal importance is the manner in which that costume is used. Individual movement, group patterning, and the colorful organization of a ceremony can make all the difference between a brilliantly costumed pageant with sensitive aesthetic qualities and a garishly arrayed group whose performance suggests a helter-skelter carnival.

This whole problem of arts degeneration is the most tragic chapter of our account, for it is unfortunately true that contact with outsiders, Indian or non-Indian, usually follows much the same pattern from tribe to tribe: a brief period of stimulation as new motifs, techniques, and materials are discovered, followed by a rapid disintegration as beliefs in the traditional concepts are undermined. Only occasionally is a bridge successfully and profitably established.

To attempt to summarize American Indian art in one paragraph is wholly impossible, for there are far too many variations in the uses of materials, aesthetic expressions, and the techniques of application. However, it is possible to assert that the greatest art of the Indian was his ability to adapt himself quickly to the environment in which he found himself, and to make major aesthetic use of the natural resources of that environment. In almost no area did he fail to make such an adjustment; while his approach to art may in some non-Indian eyes seem less sophisticated than in others, it was nonetheless a successful and satisfactory answer to the needs of his culture. To make a good life, and to satisfy the need all men have for peace of mind, security of one's home, and enrichment of one's soul is indeed a great accomplishment; most Indian cultures had met that need by the time the first Europeans arrived. That all did not make, and keep, that adjustment is only the measure of variety in approach, and an index of the differences which existed between the cultures coming into the Western Hemisphere so many centuries ago.

Wooden dance mask. Kuskwogmiut Eskimo; Kuskokwim River, Alaska. c. 1890. Length 12".

This represents Amekak, the spirit who lives in the ground. When he emerges from his hiding place, he sometimes jumps through people he does not like, leaving no mark; his victim then lies down and dies.

Walrus ivory was commonly used for many implements in the Arctic region. These small carvings illustrate the use of form and incised decoration highly developed by the Eskimo. The toggle (below) combines a fox design engraved on the body of a seal.

Carved ivories. Kuskwogmiut Eskimo; Kuskokwim River, Alaska. c. 1890. Lengths $3^1/_2$″ and $4^1/_2$″.

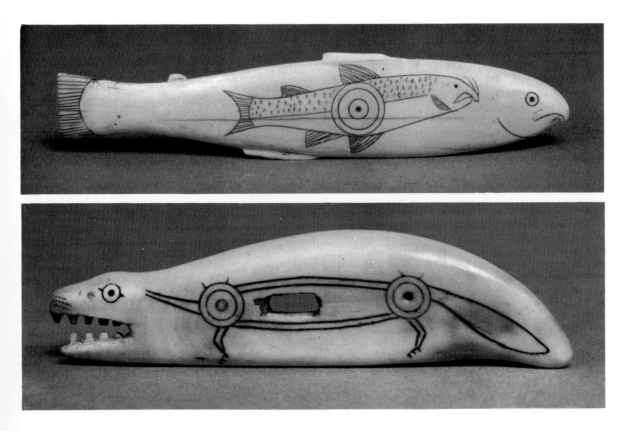

Man's shirt. Tlingit; Sitka, Alaska. c. 1900. ▶
Length 42″.

These ornate headdress pieces, trimmed in swanskin, are found among several Northwest Coast tribes, and were the property of wealthy chieftains and religious leaders. This example, portraying a beaver, has haliotis (abalone) shell inlay, and is decorated with seal whiskers. Collected c. 1890 by Lt. G. T. Emmons.

The intricate design of the famous Chilkat blankets is adapted in this garment woven of mountain goat wool and trimmed with otter fur. The symbolic representation of the brown bear is seen in the repeat motifs.

Frog woman mask. Tlingit; Gaudekan, Alaska.
c. 1850. Height 13″.

The design represents an old woman's spirit. Frogs and otters are on her face, and land spirits are carved across the forehead. This is an extremely old mask, with ship copper on the eyebrows and Russian trade buttons used for eyes. It was collected in 1880 by Lt. G. T. Emmons.

Clan helmet. Haida; Prince of Wales Island, Alaska. c. 1875. Height 9¹/₂″.

These carved wooden helmets were worn by clan leaders in ceremonies. This, representing the eagle, has swanskin and human-hair trimming. It was collected in 1880 by Lt. G. T. Emmons.

Movable mask. Kwakiutl; Vancouver Island, British Columbia, Canada. c. 1880. Length 47″.

Many of the fine carved wooden masks of the Northwest Coast peoples could be moved at will by the wearer; this mask, representing a raven, has strings which allow the dancer to impersonate that bird, opening and closing the beak as he moved about the room.

◀ Totem pole. Tlingit; Sitka, Alaska. c. 1875. Height 60′.

The custom of carving family histories was widespread on the Northwest Coast. This example demonstrates the technique of combining ancestry, clan lineage, and historical narrative in one artistic presentation.

This trio demonstrates the skill of the Northwest Coast carvers at its best. The shaman's charm (above) shows a mythological whale and its spirit; the soul-catcher (center) inlaid with haliotis (abalone) shell portrays the double-headed being Sisiutl, and is used by shamans to imprison the souls of persons. The charm carved from an elk antler (below) is the mythical sea monster who has a wolf's head; it is also inlaid with haliotis shell.

◄ Ivory carvings. Tlingit, Nootka, Niska; British Columbia, Canada. c. 1850–75. Length of longest 9″·

The finest basketry in the Indian world was produced in California by several tribes. This assortment presents a selection of several types, forms, and techniques. The weaver's command of her materials is clearly evident.

Western basketry. California and Washington. c. 1850–1900. Height of largest 18″.

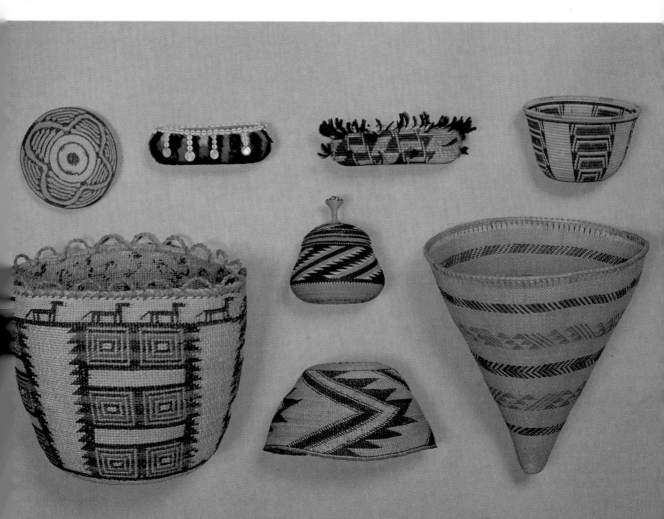

Dance club. Hunkpapa Sioux; Standing Rock, North Dakota. c. 1890. Length 35″.

This carved wand is used in the Horse Dance. The two red areas represent wounds received in battle. These dance clubs are made in a variety of forms, and each is symbolic of the purpose for which it is intended.

◄ Beadwork pouch. Cheyenne, Wyoming. c. 1875. Length 18″.

Made of buckskin, this long container was used for carrying the man's tobacco, pipe, and smoking equipment. The beads, obtained from traders, were applied to the surface in a realistic design; porcupine quilling decorates the fringes, which have brass trade bells.

Buckskin war shirt. Sans Arc Sioux; Cheyenne River, North Dakota. c. 1870. Length 34″.

The magnificence of the Plains Indian costume art is well shown in this garment. Beadwork combined with dyed porcupine quilling offers strong contrast to the painted decoration on the buckskin; so-called scalp-locks add grace to the sleeves.

Painted buffalo hide. Teton Sioux; Pine Ridge, South Dakota. c. 1865. 60 × 90″.

The use of buffalo hides as surfaces for painting is an old art among the Plains Indians. This example, of the design commonly known as "box-and-border" motif, represents the body and visceral spirit of the buffalo, as seen spread out.

By cutting and scraping away the outer layer, Indians found that a pleasing contrast could be obtained for decorating bark containers. This example demonstrates the art as applied to a *mockock*—square-sided covered container used for foodstuffs.

An early device for protecting small infants was this hooded carrier, fastened to a wooden framework. The brilliantly beaded design is offset by the use of brass grommets, obtained from traders, applied to the wooden uprights.

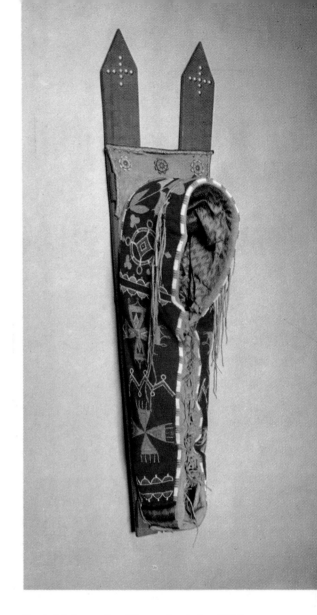

Beaded baby carrier. Kiowa; Anadarko, Oklahoma. c. 1875. Length 45".

Elm-bark *mockock*. Maniwaki Algonquin; Tineau, Quebec, Canada. c. 1900. Height 5¹/₂".

Ribbonwork appliqué. Osage; Pawhuska, Oklahoma. c. 1900. 24 × 48″.

The introduction of brilliant silks and satins made possible many new decorative techniques to the Indian craftswoman. One particularly effective art was the appliqué technique used with cut-out sections of material, sewn to a wool base obtained from traders.

The use of dyed river cane in a variety of designs is characteristic of several Southeastern Indian tribes. This motif, known to have existed since prehistoric times, shows the ability of the weaver to achieve a curvilinear design by means of geometric lacing.

Polychrome basket. Chitimacha; Louisiana. c. 1890. 6 × 6″.

Beadwork belt. Koasati; Elton, Louisiana. c. 1850. 6 × 24".

Beaded pouch. Lenni Lenape; Dewey, Oklahoma. c. 1850. Width 17".

The scroll design in this belt is found throughout many Southeastern tribes, and is representative of contemporary usage of a prehistoric motif; this same interlaced design has been found on many archaeological vessels from the region.

Not unlike the patterning seen in the ribbonwork appliqué garment (facing page), this heavily beaded shoulder pouch includes ornate ribbon trim.

A very early example of shoulder bag, made from black-dyed buckskin, decorated with porcupine quilling and dyed deer hair.

Quilled pouch. Iroquois (?) Locale unknown. c. 1750 (?) Linden Museum, Stuttgart.

Inlaid war club. Iroquois (?) Locale unknown. c. 1700 (?) National Museum, Copenhagen.

This is the typical ball-head club found throughout the Eastern Woodlands area. This superb example is one of the few remaining from such an early period; it is inlaid with *wampumpeak* in a design representing a human head. Note the carved foot.

◀ Carved mask. Seneca; Cattaraugus, New York. C. 1875. Length 11″.

This Spoon Mouth mask is used in False Face ceremonies, held as curing rituals. Many varieties and styles exist, but all follow the general style illustrated here.

Made of black-dyed deerskin, decorated in a floral design by means of dyed moose hair, this pair of man's moccasins clearly reflects the influence of the French convents, where young girls were taught the art of sewing. Although the design is new, the style is old.

Buckskin moccasins. Huron; Lorette, Quebec, Canada. c. 1825. Length 9″.

Woven wool blanket. Navajo; New Mexico. c. 1880. 77 × 91″.

Of the design commonly termed a "chief's blanket," although no such distinction actually exists, this is unusual for its size as well as for the tightness of weave.

◀ Painted coat. Naskapi; Labrador, Newfoundland, Canada. c. 1800 (?) Length 43″.

The cut of this tailored garment clearly indicates European influence, but the decorative design is aboriginal. The pigment was obtained from native berries.

Silver necklace, buckle, and brooch. Navajo; Arizona. c. 1935–1960. Buckle 2¹/₂ × 3″, brooch 3¹/₂″, necklace 14″.

The art of working in silver is not an old one among the Navajo; the earliest references seem to place it at about 1853. These examples illustrate three techniques: the so-called squash blossom necklace is made of hollow soldered beads, with a cast pendant. The cast buckle was formed in a carved stone mold, while the scallop-edged disc *còncho* is hammered and stamped.

Basketry group. Hopi; Shungopovi, Arizona. White Mountain Apache; Arizona. Hopi; Oraibi, Arizona. c. 1900. Diameter of largest 16″.

Three styles of Southwestern basketry weaving are illustrated in this trio: wicker weave, twining, and coiled work. The flat platters are used for decoration and for cornmeal; the larger container is a storage basket.

243

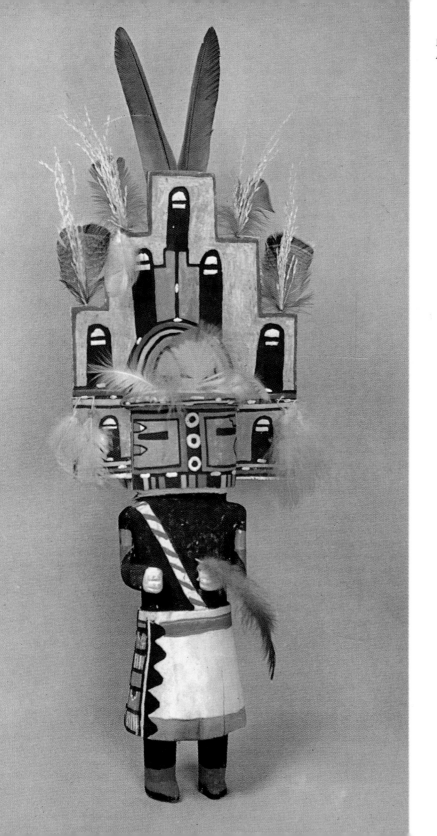

Kachina dolls. Hopi; Second Mesa, Arizona. c. 1925. Height of tallest 25″.

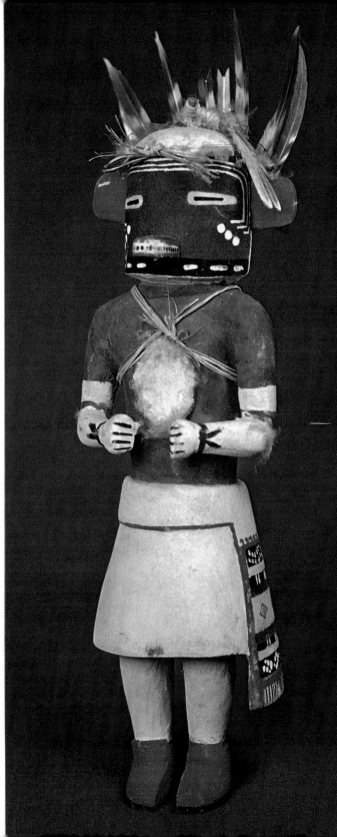

Known as *tihü* to the Hopi Indians, these are both educational and economical items representing the spirit beings of the people. Effigies of human performers wearing painted masks, these colorful figurines are well known to art connoisseurs. The smaller figurine is Laqán Kachina, the Squirrel Being; the taller is the Hümis Kachina performer, who usually appears at the Nimán Ceremony in the spring.

Pottery vessels. Hopi, Arizona; Zia, New Mexico; Zuñi, New Mexico. c. 1900. Height of tallest 9″.

A wide variety of pottery is made throughout the pueblo villages of the Southwest. These three demonstrate something of the extremes in style, design, and finish.

Watercolor painting *The Food Bearers*. San Ildefonso Pueblo, New Mexico. c. 1960. 17 × 26″.

An art often overlooked is that of painting in watercolors. Although the contemporary form is largely an introduced art, the custom of painting in flat colors on a clay surface goes back to prehistoric times in the Southwest. This is by Gilbert Atencio, one of the most promising younger artists.

Dance mask. Yaqui; Sonora, Mexico. c. 1900. ▶
Length 8″.

Worn by the *Pascolero* dancers, this is
carved of soft wood, trimmed with
horsehair, and painted.

Woven garment. Quiché Maya; Chichicastenango, Guatemala. c. 1900. Width 35″.

A carry-over of the ancient Maya weaving arts, this woman's *huípil* is a colorful example of strong textile design.

Appliqué blouse. Cuna; San Blas Islands, Panama. c. 1925. Length 25″.

Similar to sewn appliqué work found among the Seminole and Osage, this *mola* is characteristic of the textile arts of the San Blas women.

These figurines are used in curing ceremonies, then thrown away once they have served their purpose. Designs vary greatly; this represents a European.

Carved effigy. Cuna; San Blas Islands, Panama. c. 1925. Height 20″.

Feather ornaments. Urubú; Caninde, Brazil. c. 1960. Length of central piece 11″.

The use of brilliantly hued tropical bird feathers for body decoration is widespread in South America. These represent some of the best of that work: a necklace, a man's bone whistle, and a chin ornament.

Man's blouse. Mayoruna; Rio Marañón, Peru. c. 1925. 45 × 45".

The *cushma*, a loose overblouse similar to a *poncho*, is typical of lowland South America. This painted cotton garment bears the design common to a large area of the region; the linear pattern is found in textiles, woodwork, and pottery.

This has a design similar to the *cushma* on the facing page and is made by people whose language is also similar.

Liquor vessel. Conibo; Upper Amazon River, Peru. c. 1925. Height 25 1/2".

Feather mask. Tapirapé; Rio Tapirapé, Brazil. c. 1960. Height 31″.

Commonly known as a *Cara Grande*, this is worn in harvest festivities, when the Banana Fiesta is held. These huge wooden masks are covered with pitch, to which feathers are attached; white clay completes the design. The eyes are of shell.

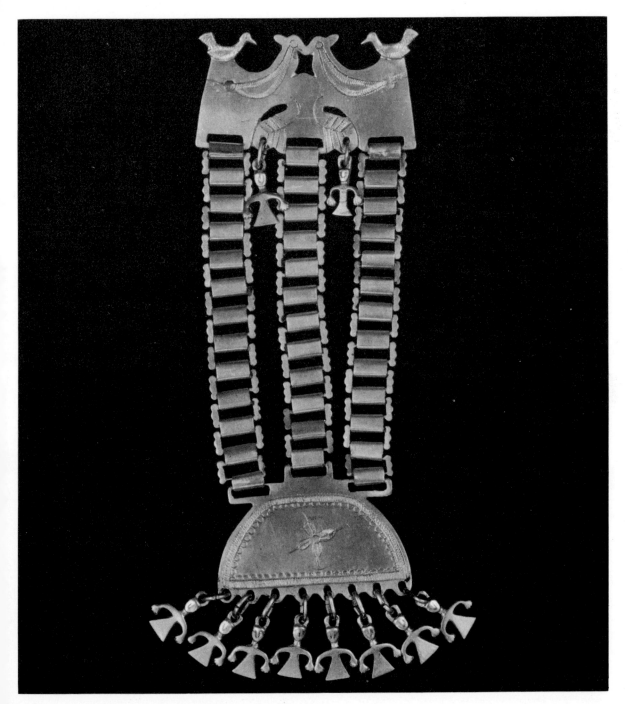

Breast ornament. Mapuche; Santiago, Chile. c. 1900. Length 10″.

The *siquel* is a breast ornament made of heavy silver, traditionally worn by women throughout the Araucanian region. The design combines both prehistoric and European motifs.

Bibliography

THE ANCIENT CIVILIZATIONS AND THE MEXICAN CULTURES

The Aztec hymns from a manuscript in the Biblioteca Nacional were translated and annotated by LEONHARD SCHULTZE-JENA, and, after his death, edited by GERDT KUTSCHER in *Quellenwerke zur alten Geschichte Amerikas*, VI, Stuttgart, 1957

ANTON, FERDINAND, *Mexico, Indianerkunst aus präkolumbischer Zeit*, Munich, 1961

ANTON, FERDINAND, nos. 23, 24, 25 in *The Art of Writing* (catalogue of an exhibition in fifty panels), Baden-Baden, 1965 (UNESCO publication)

BERNAL, IGNACIO, *Mexico: pre-Hispanic Paintings*, preface by Jacques Soustelle, New York, 1958

BURLAND, COTTIE A., *Art and Life in Ancient Mexico*, Oxford, 1948

BURLAND, COTTIE A., *Man and Art*, London and New York, 1959

BURLAND, COTTIE A., *The Selden Roll, an Ancient Mexican Picture Manuscript*, Berlin, 1955

CASO, ALFONSO, *Calendario y Escritura de las antiguas Culturas de Monte Albán*, Mexico, 1947

CASO, ALFONSO, *People of the Sun*, Norman, Okla., 1958

CASO, ALFONSO, and BERNAL, IGNACIO, *Urnas de Oaxaca*, Mexico, 1952

Codex Vindobonensis Mexicanus I, Akademische Druck- und Verlagsanstalt, Graz, 1963

COVARRUBIAS, MIGUEL, *Indian Art of Mexico and Central America*, New York, 1957

COVARRUBIAS, MIGUEL, *Mexico South*, New York, 1947

DIAZ DEL CASTILLO, BERNAL, *The Discovery and Conquest of the New World, 1517–1521*, New York, 1958

Die Geschichte der Königreiche von Colhuacan und Mexico, text with translation by WALTER LEHMANN. Stuttgart and Berlin, 1938

DIGBY, ADRIAN, and BUSHNELL, GEOFFREY H. S., *Ancient American Pottery*, London, 1955

DISSELHOFF, HANS DIETER, *Geschichte der altamerikanischen Kulturen*, Munich, 1953

DISSELHOFF, HANS DIETER, and LINNE, SIGVALD, *Alt-Amerika* (Kunst der Welt), Baden-Baden, 1960

DOCKSTADER, FREDERICK J., *Indian Art in Middle America*, Greenwich, Conn., 1964

DRUCKER, PHILIP, "La Venta, Tabasco: A Study of Olmec Ceramics and Art," in *Bulletin of the Bureau of American Ethnology*, Vol. CLIII, Washington, D.C., 1952

DRUCKER, PHILIP, HEIZER, ROBERT F., and SQUIER, ROBERT J., "Excavations at La Venta, 1955," in *Bulletin of the Bureau of American Ethnology*, Vol. CLXX, Washington, D.C., 1959

EMMERICH, ANDRE, *Art before Columbus*, New York, 1963

ENCISO, JORGE, *Design Motifs of Ancient Mexico*, Mexico, 1947, and New York, 1953

Esplendor del México Antiguo, ed. CARMEN COOK DE LEONARD, Mexico, 1959, 2 vols.

FEUCHTWANGER, FRANZ, *The Art of Ancient Mexico*, with photographs by Irmgard Groth-Kimball, London, 1958

KATZ, FRIEDRICH, *Die sozialökonomischen Verhältnisse bei den Azteken im 15. und 16. Jahrhundert;* translation in English, *Past and Present*, XIII: 14–25, London, 1958

KELEMEN, PAL, *Medieval American Art*, New York, 1956, 2 vols.

KRICKEBERG, WALTER, *Märchen der Azteken und Inka-Peruaner, Maya und Muisca*, Jena, 1928

KRICKEBERG, WALTER, *Las antiguas culturas mexicanas*, translated by S. Garst and J. Reuter, Mexico, 1961

KUBLER, GEORGE, *The Art and Architecture of Ancient America*, Baltimore, 1962

KUTSCHER, GERDT, *Präkolumbische Kunst aus Mexico und Mittelamerika*, Exhibition Catalogue, Munich, 1958

LEHMANN, H., *Pre-Columbian Ceramics*, London, 1961

LEHMANN, WALTER, *The History of Ancient Mexican Art*, New York, 1922

LOTHROP, S. K., *Treasures of Ancient America: the Arts of the Pre-Columbian Civilizations from Mexico to Peru*, Geneva, 1964

LOTHROP, S. K., and others, *Pre-Columbian Art (Robert Woods Bliss Collection)*, London, 1957

MARQUINA, I., *Arquitectura prehispánica*, Mexico, 1964

MEDIONI, GILBERT, and PINTO, MARIE-THERESE, *Art in Ancient Mexico*, New York, 1941

Middle American Research Records, New Orleans, 1942–1950, 1961

NICHOLSON, IRENE, *Firefly in the Night: A Study of Ancient Mexican Poetry and Symbolism*, London, 1959

NOWOTNY, KARL A., "Der Codex Becker II," in *Archiv für Völkerkunde*, Vienna, 1957

NOWOTNY, KARL A., "Der Codex Becker I (Le Manuscrit du Cacique)," in *Archiv für Völkerkunde*, Vienna, 1959

NOWOTNY, KARL A., "Die Bilderfolge des Codex Vindobonensis und verwandter Handschriften," in *Archiv für Völkerkunde*, Vienna, 1959

NOWOTNY, KARL A., "Erläuterungen zum Codex Vindobonensis (Vorderseite)," in *Archiv für Völkerkunde*, Vienna, 1948

NOWOTNY, KARL A., *Tlacuilolli, die mexikanischen Bilderschriften Stil und Inhalt*, Berlin, 1961

PETERSON, F. A., *Ancient Mexico*, New York and London, 1959

PIJOAN, JOSE, *Arte Precolombino, Mexicano y Maya* (Summa Artis: Historia General del Arte, Vol. X), Madrid, 1952

PORTILLA, MIGUEL LEON, *Aztec Thought and Culture*, Norman, Okla., 1963

PORTILLA, MIGUEL LEON, *Rückkehr der Götter*, Cologne and Opladen, 1962, Leipzig, 1964

ROBERTSON, DONALD, *Pre-Columbian Architecture,* New York, 1963

SCHLENTHER, URSULA, "Über die Auflösung der Theokratien im präkolumbischen Amerika," in *Ethnographisch-Archäologische Zeitschrift,* Berlin, 1961

SEJOURNE, LAURETTE, *Burning Water; Thought and Religion in Ancient Mexico,* New York, 1957

SELER, EDUARD, *Gesammelte Abhandlungen zur amerikanischen Sprach- und Altertumskunde,* Berlin 1903–1923, 5 vols.; new ed. Graz, 1960–1962

SOUSTELLE, JACQUES, *The Daily Life of the Aztecs on the Eve of the Spanish Conquest,* translated by P. O'Brian, London, 1961

SOUSTELLE, JACQUES, *Arts of Ancient Mexico,* London, 1967

SPRATLING, WILLIAM, *More Human than Divine,* Mexico, 1960

TOSCANO, SALVADOR, *Arte Precolombino de Mexico,* Mexico, 1952, 2 vols.

TRIMBORN, HERMANN, *Das alte Amerika* (Grosse Kulturen der Frühzeit), Stuttgart, 1959

VAILLANT, GEORGE C., *Aztecs of Mexico,* Garden City, N.Y., 1962

WAUCHOPE, ROBERT, *Implications of Radiocarbon Dates from Middle and South America,* Middle American Research Institute (II: 2, 19–39, 1954), Tulane University, New Orleans

WESTHEIM, PAUL, *The Art of Ancient Mexico,* translated by U. Bernard, Garden City, N.Y., 1965

WESTHEIM, PAUL, *Ideas fundamentales del arte prehispánico en México,* Mexico, 1957

WESTHEIM, PAUL, *The Sculpture of Ancient Mexico,* Garden City, N.Y., 1963

WOLF, ERIC R., *Sons of the Shaking Earth,* Chicago, 1959

MAYA CULTURE

The Annals of the Cakchiquels, translated by A. Recina and D. Goetz, Norman, Okla., 1953

Ancient Maya Paintings of Bonampak, Mexico (Carnegie Institute of Washington), Washington, D.C., 1955

ANDERS, F., *Das Pantheon der Maya,* Graz, 1963

ANTON, FERDINAND, *Maya, Indianische Kunst aus Mittelamerika,* Munich, 1965

ANTON, FERDINAND, *Kunst der Maya,* Leipzig, 1967

BARTHEL, T. S., *Die gegenwärtige Situation in der Erforschung der Mayaschrift,* Copenhagen, 1958

BRAINERD, G. W., *The Maya Civilization,* Los Angeles, 1954

CHINCHILLA, C. S., *Aproximación al Arte Maya,* Guatemala, 1964

Codex Dresden, Die Maya-Handschrift der Sächsischen Landesbibliothek Dresden, Dresden, 1962

CORDAN, W., *Götter und Göttertiere der Maya: Resultate des Mérida-Systems,* Berne and Munich, 1963

DECKERT, H., *Maya-Handschrift der Sächsischen Landesbibliothek Dresden: Codex Dresdensis – Geschichte und Bibliographie,* Berlin, 1963

DIESELDORFF, E. P., *Kunst und Religion der Mayavölker im alten und heutigen Mittelamerika,* Berlin, 1926–1933

DUBY, G., *Chiapas indígena,* Mexico, 1961

Examples of Maya Pottery in the [*University of Pennsylvania*] *Museum and Other Collections,* ed. G. B. GORDON and J. A. MASON, Philadelphia, 1925–1943, 3 vols.

FÖRSTERMANN, E., *Die Maya-Handschrift der Königlichen Bibliothek zu Dresden.* Leipzig, 1880

GALLENKAMP, CHARLES, *Maya,* New York, 1959

HABERLAND, W., *Die regionale Verteilung von Schmuckelementen im Bereich der klassischen Maya-Kulturen,* Hamburg, 1953

KIMBALL, IRMGARD GROTH-, *Maya Terrakotten,* Tübingen, 1960

The Maya and Their Neighbors, New York, 1940, repr. 1962

MENGIN, E., *Die wichtigsten Ergebnisse der Mayasprachforschung,* Vienna, 1962

MORLEY, SYLVANUS G., *The Ancient Maya,* Stanford, Calif., 1956

NOWOTNY, KARL A., *Die Konkordanz der mesoamerikanischen Chronologie,* Braunschweig, 1951

PAVON ABREU, R., *Bonampak en la escultura,* Mexico, 1962

POLLOCK, H. E. D., *Mayapan, Yucatan, Mexico,* Washington, D.C., 1962

PROSKOURIAKOFF, TATIANA A., *An Album of Maya Architecture,* Norman, Okla., 1963

PROSKOURIAKOFF, TATIANA A., *A Study of Classic Maya Sculpture* (Carnegie Institute of Washington Publication), Washington, D.C., 1950

RUZ, L., *La Civilización de los antiguos Mayas,* Mexico, 1963

SCHLENTHER, U., *Die geistige Welt der Maya: Einführung in die Schriftzeugnisse einer indianischen Priesterkultur,* Berlin, 1965

SCHULTZE-JENA, L., *Indiana I: Leben, Glaube und Sprache der Quiché von Guatemala,* Jena, 1933

SODI, D. M., *La Literatura de los Mayas,* Mexico, 1964

Teatro indígena prehispánico (Rabinal Cichi), Mexico, 1955

THOMPSON, J. E. S., *A Correlation of Mayan and European Calendars,* Chicago, 1927

THOMPSON, J. E. S., *The Rise and Fall of Maya Civilization,* Norman, Okla., 1966

THOMPSON, J. E. S., *Systems of Hieroglyphic Writing in Middle America and Methods of Deciphering Them,* Salt Lake City, 1959

WADEPUHL, W., *Die alten Maya und ihre Kultur,* Leipzig, 1964

WILLEY, G. R., "The Structure of Ancient Maya Society," in *American Anthropologist,* n. s. Vol. LVIII (Menasha, Wisc.), pp. 777–782

ZIMMERMANN, G., *Die Hieroglyphen der Maya-Handschriften,* Hamburg, 1956

THE LANDS OF GOLD (FROM NICARAGUA TO COLOMBIA)

ACUNA, LUIS ALBERTO, *El arte de los indios colombianos,* Mexico, 1942

BENNETT, WENDELL C., *Archaeological Regions of Colombia: a Ceramic Survey* (Yale University Publications in Anthropology, No. 30), New Haven, 1944

DOCKSTADER, FREDERICK J., *Indian Art in Middle America,* Greenwich, Conn., 1964

DUQUE GOMEZ, LUIS, *Colombia: Monumentos históricos y arqueológicos,* Mexico, 1955, 2 vols.

NACHTIGALL, HORST, *Alt-Kolumbien: Vorgeschichtliche Indianerkulturen,* Berlin, 1961

NACHTIGALL, HORST, *Die amerikanischen Megalithkulturen,* Berlin, 1958

NACHTIGALL, HORST, *Indianerkunst der Nord-Anden,* Berlin, 1961

NACHTIGALL, HORST, *Tierradentro: Archäologie und Ethnographie einer kolumbianischen Landschaft,* Zurich, 1955

PEREZ DE BARRADAS, JOSE, *Orfebrería prehispánica de Colombia: Estilo Calima,* Madrid, 1958, 2 vols.

STONE, DORIS, *Introduction to the Archaeology of Costa Rica,* San José, 1958

TRIMBORN, HERMANN, *Vergessene Königreiche: Studien zur Völkerkunde und Altertumskunde Nordwest-Kolumbiens,* Braunschweig, 1948

PERU

ANTON, FERDINAND, *Alt-Peru und seine Kunst,* Leipzig, 1962

ANTON, FERDINAND, *Peru, Indianerkunst aus präkolumbischer Zeit,* Munich, 1958

BAUDIN, LOUIS, *A Socialist Empire; the Incas of Peru,* translated by K. Woods, Princeton, 1961

BAUDIN, LOUIS, *So lebten die Inkas,* Stuttgart, 1957

BAUDIN, LOUIS, *Daily Life in Peru,* London, 1960

BAUDIN, LOUIS, *Les Incas,* Paris, 1964

BENNETT, WENDELL C., *Ancient Arts of the Andes,* New York, 1954

BENNETT, WENDELL C., and BIRD, JUNIUS A., *Andean Culture History,* New York, 1960

BINGHAM, H., *Lost City of the Incas,* New York, 1948

BIRD, J., and BELLINGER, L., *Paracas Fabrics and Nazca Needlework, Peruvian Textiles,* Washington, D.C., 1954

BUSHNELL, G. H. S., *Peru,* New York, 1957

DISSELHOFF, H. D., *Alt-Peru,* Exhibition Catalogue, Cologne, 1959

DISSELHOFF, H. D., *Geschichte der altamerikanischen Kulturen,* Munich, 1953

DISSELHOFF, H. D., *Gott muss Peruaner sein,* Wiesbaden, 1956

DOCKSTADER, FREDERICK J., *Indian Art in South America,* Greenwich, Conn., 1967

DRÄGER, L., *Das alte Peru: aus dem Museum für Völkerkunde, Leipzig,* Leipzig, 1964

ENGEL, F., "Early Sites in the Pisco Valley of Peru – Tambo Colorado," in *American Antiquity,* Vol. 23, 1957

ENGEL, F., "Early Sites on the Peruvian Coast," in *Southwestern Journal of Anthropology,* Vol. 13, 1957

ENGL, LISELOTTE, *Die Traumgeschichte des Inca Huayna Capac: Peru und Ecuador im XV. und XVI. Jahrhundert* (in preparation)

ENGL, LIŠELOTTE, *Huayna Capac, Atahuallpa und Huascar, Untersuchungen zur Geschichte der letzten Jahrzehnte des Incareiches* (Dissertation), Munich, 1954

GALLO, M., *Gold in Peru,* Recklinghausen, 1959

GARCILASO DE LA VEGA, EL INCA, *Royal Commentaries of the Incas,* Austin, Texas, 1966

Handbook of South American Indians, ed. J. H. STEWART, Washington, D. C., 1947

HEYERDAHL, THOR, *Kon-Tiki,* New York and London, 1950

HORKHEIMER, H., *Nahrung und Nahrungsgewinn im vorspanischen Peru* (Ibero-Americana 2), Berlin, 1960

HUMBOLDT, A. VON, *Vues des Cordillères et monuments des peuples indigènes de l'Amérique,* Paris, 1810

KARSTEN, R., *Das altperuanische Inkareich und seine Kultur,* Leipzig, 1949

KAUFFMANN-DOIG, F., *El Perú antiguo,* Lima, 1963

KAUFFMANN-DOIG, F., *La cultura Chavín,* Lima, 1963

KAUFFMANN-DOIG, F., *Los fundamentos de la investigación del Perú arqueológico,* Lima, 1963

KAUFFMANN-DOIG, F., *Origen de la cultura peruana,* Lima, 1963

KAUFFMANN-DOIG, F., VALEGA, J. M., et al., *Historia del Perú desde sus origines hasta el presente,* Lima, 1962–1963, 3 vols.

KROEBER, A. L., *Paracas Cavernas and Chavín* (University of California Publications in American Archaeology and Ethnology, Vol. 40), Berkeley and Los Angeles, Calif., 1953

KUTSCHER, G., *Chimu, eine altperuanische Hochkultur,* Berlin, 1950

LARCO HOYLE, R., *Cronologia arqueológica del norte del Perú,* Trujillo and Buenos Aires, 1948

LARCO HOYLE, R., *Los Cupisniques,* Lima, 1941

LARCO HOYLE, R., *Los Mochicas,* Lima, 1938–1939, 2 vols.

LEHMANN, WALTER, and UBBELOHDE-DOERING, H., *The Art of Old Peru,* London, 1924

LEICHT, H., *Pre-Inca Art and Culture,* New York, 1960

LEUZINGER, E., *Die Kunst von Alt-Peru (Alt-Peru aus Schweizer Sammlungen),* Exhibition Catalogue of the Kunsthaus, Zurich, 1957

LOTHROP, S. K., *Inca Treasure as Depicted by Spanish Historians,* Los Angeles, 1938

MASON, J. A., *The Ancient Civilization of Peru,* London, 1957

MEANS, PHILIP A., *Fall of the Inca Empire and the Spanish Rule in Peru, 1530–1780,* New York, 1932

RYDEN, S., *Andean Excavation,* Stockholm, 1957

RYDEN, S., *Archaeological Researches in the Highlands of Bolivia,* Göteborg, 1947

SAWYER, A. R., *The Nathan Cummings Collection of Ancient Peruvian Art (The Art Institute of Chicago),* Chicago, 1954

TRIMBORN, H., *Das alte Amerika,* Stuttgart, 1959

TRIMBORN, H., *Die Religionen der Völkerschaften des südlichen Mittelamerikas und des nördlichen und mittleren Andenraums,* Stuttgart, 1961

UBBELOHDE-DOERING, H., *Der Gallinazo-Stil und die Chronologie der alt-peruanischen Frühkulturen,* Munich, 1957

UBBELOHDE-DOERING, H., *Alt-Mexikanische und Peruanische Malerei,* Berlin, 1959

UBBELOHDE-DOERING, H., *Auf der Königstrasse der Inka,* Berlin, 1941

UBBELOHDE-DOERING, H., *Kunst im Reich der Inka,* Tübingen, 1952

UHLE, M., *Die alten Kulturen Perus im Hinblick auf die Archäologie und Geschichte des amerikanischen Kontinents,* Berlin, 1935

VALCARCEL, L. E., *Machu Picchu: el más famoso monumento arqueológico del Perú.* Buenos Aires, 1964

VON HAGEN, V. W., *The Ancient Sun-Kingdoms of the Americas,* Cleveland, 1961

VON HAGEN, V. W., *The Desert Kingdoms of Peru,* Greenwich, Conn., 1965

WILLEY, G. R., *A Middle Period Cemetery in Virú Valley,* Washington, D.C., 1947

INDIAN TRIBAL ART

AMSDEN, CHARLES, *Navajo Weaving, Its Technic and History,* Santa Ana, 1934

BARBEAU, MARIUS, *Haida Carvers in Argillite,* Ottawa, 1957

BARBEAU, MARIUS, *Haida Myths Illustrated in Argillite Carvings,* Ottawa, 1953

BARBEAU, MARIUS, *Totem Poles,* Ottawa, 1930, 2 vols.

BURNETT, E. K., *The Spiro Mound Collection in the Museum,* New York, 1945

CHRISTENSEN, ERWIN O., *Primitive Art,* New York, 1955

COLLINS, HENRY B., *Prehistoric Art of the Alaskan Eskimo,* Washington, D.C., 1929

COVARRUBIAS, MIGUEL, *The Eagle, the Jaguar, and the Serpent,* New York, 1954

CURTIS, E. S., *The North American Indian,* Cambridge, Mass., 1903–1930, 30 vols.

DAVIS, ROBERT, *Native Arts of the Pacific Northwest,* Stanford, Calif., 1949

DUNN, DOROTHY, *The Development of Modern American Indian Painting: Southwest and Plains Area,* Santa Fe, N.M., 1951

DOCKSTADER, FREDERICK J., *Indian Art in America,* Greenwich, Conn., 1962

DOCKSTADER, FREDERICK J., *Kunst in Amerika: I,* Stuttgart, 1965

DOCKSTADER, FREDERICK J., *The Kachina and the White Man,* Bloomfield Hills, Mich., 1954

DOUGLAS, FREDERIC H., and D'HARNONCOURT, RENE, *Indian Art of the United States,* Exhibition Catalogue of the Museum of Modern Art, New York, 1941

D'HARCOURT, RAOUL, *Arts de l'Amérique,* Paris, 1948

EWERS, JOHN C., *Plains Indian Painting,* Stanford, Calif., 1939

EWERS, JOHN C., *Blackfeet Crafts,* Washington, D.C., 1945

FUNDABURK, EMMA LILA, and FOREMAN, MARY DOUGLASS, *Sun Circles and Human Hands,* Luverne, Ala., 1957

HABERLAND, WOLFGANG, *Nordamerika – Indianer – Eskimo – Westindien* (Kunst der Welt), Baden-Baden, 1965

HEYE, GEORGE G., *Certain Aboriginal Artifacts from San Miguel Island, California,* New York, 1921

HOFFMAN, WILLIAM J., *The Graphic Art of the Eskimos,* Washington, D.C., 1895

INVERARITY, R. BRUCE, *Art of the Northwest Coast Indians,* Berkeley, Calif., 1950

KELEMAN, PAL, *Mediaeval American Art,* New York, 1956

KROEBER, ALFRED LOUIS, *Cultural and Natural Areas of Native North America,* Berkeley, Calif., 1939

LINTON, RALPH C., "Primitive Art," in *Kenyon Review,* Vol. III (Jan. 1941), pp. 34–51

MALLERY, GARRICK, *Pictographs of the North American Indians* (Bureau of American Ethnology, Annual Report IV), Washington, D. C., 1886

MALLERY, GARRICK, *Picture Writing of the American Indians* (Bureau of American Ethnology, Annual Report X), Washington, D.C., 1893

MASON, J. ALDEN, *Eskimo Pictorial Art,* Philadelphia, 1927

MASON, OTIS T., *Aboriginal American Basketry,* Washington, D. C., 1902

MERA, HARRY P., *Indian Silverwork of the Southwest,* Globe, Ariz., 1959

MERA, HARRY P., *Style Trends of Pueblo Pottery in the Rio Grande and Little Colorado Cultural Areas from the 16th to the 19th Centuries,* Santa Fe, N.M., 1939

MOOREHEAD, WARREN K., *Stone Ornaments of the American Indians,* Andover, Mass., 1917

MOOREHEAD, WARREN K., *The Stone Age in North America,* Boston, 1910, 2 vols.

ORCHARD, WILLIAM C., *Beads and Beadwork of the American Indians,* New York, 1929

SHETRONE, HENRY CLYDE, *The Mound Builders,* New York, 1930

SIDES, DOROTHY, *Decorative Art of the Southwestern Indians,* Santa Ana, Calif., 1936

SPECK, FRANK G., *The Iroquois,* Bloomfield Hills, Mich., 1965

STEWARD, JULIAN H., *Petroglyphs of California and Adjoining States,* Berkeley and Washington, D. C., 1929

SYDOW, ECKART VON, *Die Kunst der Naturvölker und der Vorzeit,* Berlin, 1923

TANNER, CLARA LEE, *Southwest Indian Painting,* Tucson, Ariz., 1957

UNDERHILL, RUTH M., *Pueblo Crafts,* Washington, D. C., 1944

VAILLANT, GEORGE CLAPP, *Indian Arts in North America,* New York, 1939

WEST, GEORGE, *Tobacco Pipes and Smoking Customs of the American Indians,* Milwaukee, 1934

WILDSCHUT, WILLIAM, and EWERS, JOHN C., *Crow Indian Beadwork: a Descriptive and Historical Study,* New York, 1959

WINGERT, PAUL S., *American Indian Sculpture,* New York, 1949

The authors and publisher wish to thank all those who made this volume possible, and in particular the directors of the various museums, the private collectors, and the photographers.

Index

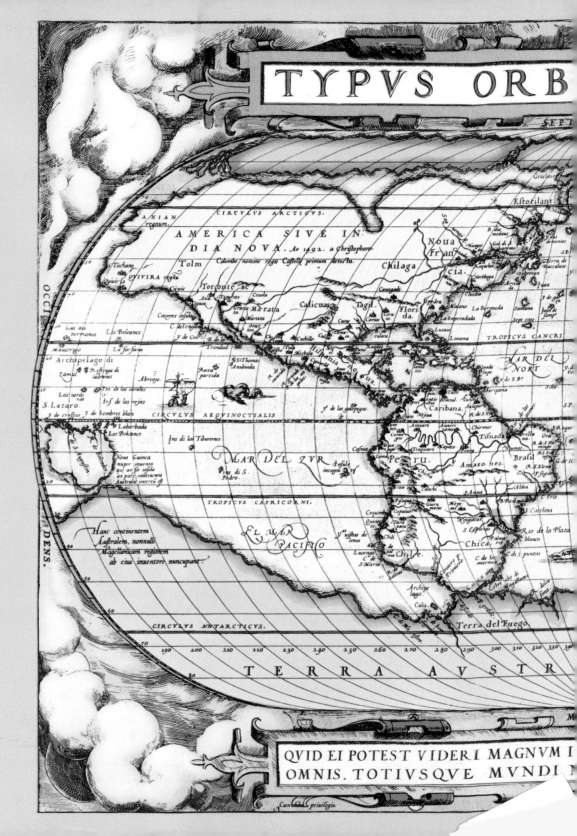